ber & Bead Jewelry

utiful Designs to Make & Wear

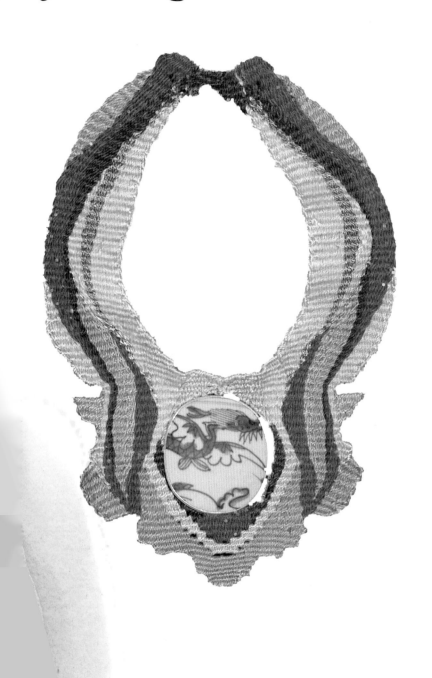

Fereshteh's Fantasy: *Commissioned by Fereshteh Klaus of Washington, DC. Incorporates old linen threads from a friend's attic plus old Japanese crumb glass beads, red whiteheart beads, and gold dangles from Thailand.*

Fiber & Bead Jewelry
Beautiful Designs to Make & Wear

Helen Banes
with
Sally Banes

Sterling Publishing Co., Inc. New York

A Sterling / Chapelle Book

Chapelle:

Jo Packham, Owner

Cathy Sexton, Design and Layout Editor

Staff: Marie Barber, Ann Bear, Areta Bingham, Kass Burchett, Marilyn Goff, Holly Hollingsworth, Susan Jorgensen, Barbara Milburn, Linda Orton, Karmen Quinney, Leslie Ridenour, Cindy Stoeckl, Gina Swapp

Photographers: Martin Amt, Mt. Rainier, MD; William Allen, Alexandria, VA; Joel Breger/PRS Associates, Inc., Kensington, MD; Mark Gulezian/Quicksilver, Takoma Park, MD; Roy Karten, Silver Spring, MD; Joan Menard, Annandale, VA; Richard Rodriguez, Arlington, VA

Specialty products recommended by author and used in models of projects herein include: beading pins, size 14, 7/8"—Prym Dritz Corp., P.O. Box 75715, Charlotte, NC 28275; warp thread (Irish waxed linen carpet thread), spools available in 18 colors, 2- and 3-ply—Royalwood, Inc., 517 Woodville Road, Mansfield, OH 44907 (800) 526-1630; weft thread, DMC perle cotton #3; and a wide variety of others; metallic threads, Kreinik; tapestry needles, #18 and #20; nylon monofilament, #8.

If you have any questions or comments or would like information on specialty products featured in this book, please contact Chapelle, Ltd., Inc., P.O. Box 9252, Ogden, UT 84409 • (801) 621-2777 • (801) 621-2788 Fax • e-mail: chapelle@chapelleltd.com / website: www.chapelleltd.com

Library of Congress Cataloging-in-Publication Data Available

10 9 8 7 6 5 4 3 2 1

First paperback edition published in 2002 by
Sterling Publishing Company
387 Park Avenue South, New York, NY 10016
©2000 by Helen Barnes
Distributed in Canada by Sterling Publishing
c/o Canadian Manda Group, One Atlantic Avenue, Suite 105
Toronto, Ontario, Canada M6K 3E7
Distributed in Australia by Capricorn Link (Australia) Pty Ltd.
P.O. Box 704, Windsor, NSW 2756, Australia
Printed in China
All rights reserved

Sterling ISBN 0-8069-6082-5 Hardcover
        ISBN 1-4027-0073-3 Paperback

Mendocino Madness:
Necklace created during a collaboratively taught workshop at the Mendocino Art Center in Mendocino, California. Segmented polymer clay figure made by Tory Hughes.

table of Contents

This book is dedicated to the generations
of influential men in my family:

my late father, Morris Richter,
a textile worker who carried
his cutting machine on his shoulder;
I followed the family tradition

my husband, Daniel Banes,
a true Renaissance man;
patriarch of the family

my sons-in-law,
Larry Harris, Dawa Sherpa,
and Noël Carroll,
who have contributed to
the diversity of our clan

my grandsons,
Joe Bell, Panama Bartholomy,
and Steve Kirstein,
who have traveled in new directions

Blessed are my great-grandchildren,
Zachary, Kylie, and Richard Kirstein—
for they shall inherit the beads!

Cravat:
*Neckpiece commissioned by
John Marshall of Oakland,
California, incorporating
elements from India.
Center element of
polymer clay
by Tory Hughes.
Glass bead as a slide
made by Don Schneider.*

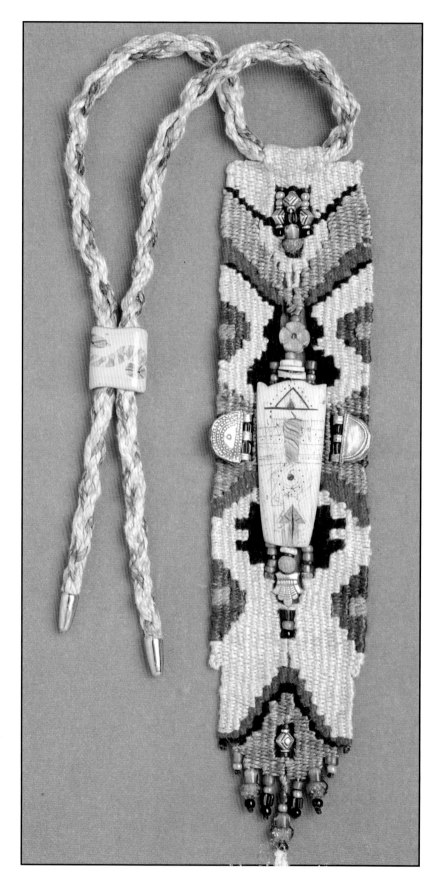

About Helen Banes

HELEN BANES is a fiber artist and jewelry designer. Born in Chicago in 1920, she has studied at the University of Maryland and Parsons School of Design. She is a founding member of Fiberworks Gallery in Alexandria, Virginia, and the founding president of the Bead Society of Greater Washington. A desire to incorporate beads and other perforated objects into her woven pieces led to her most important artistic innovation: the method of stringing beads on a double warp, using a shaped loom on a lightweight portable board.

Helen Banes has given lectures and taught workshops at numerous galleries, museums, schools, and centers, including the Smithsonian Institution (Washington, DC), Art League Schools (Alexandria, VA), Palm Springs Desert Museum (Palm Springs, CA), Textile Museum (Washington, DC), Textile Arts Centre (Chicago, IL), Bead Designers International (Boston, MA), Mendocino Art Center (Mendocino, CA), Teton Science School (Jackson Hole, WY), Linekona Academy Art Center (Honolulu, HI), and Centre pour Arts Visuelles (Montreal, Canada). Her work has been featured in articles in *Ornament Magazine, Flying Needle,* and *Threads*, and her necklaces have been exhibited at the Renwick Gallery and the Smithsonian Traveling Exhibition.

About Sally Banes

SALLY BANES is Marian Hannah Winter Professor of Theatre History and Dance Studies at the University of Wisconsin–Madison. Her books include *Terpsichore in Sneakers: Post-Modern Dance; Democracy's Body: Judson Dance Theater 1962–64; Writing Dancing in the Age of Postmodernism; Dancing Women: Female Bodies on Stage;* and *Subversive Expectations: Performance Art and Paratheater in New York 1976–85*. She has edited several books, including *Sweet Home Chicago: The Real City Guide* and *Soviet Choreographers in the 1920s* (by Elizabeth Souritz), and she is the director and producer of the documentary video *The Last Conversation: Eisenstein's Carmen Ballet*. She is a past president of the Society of Dance History Scholars and the Dance Critics Association.

Helen's work reflects the times. Recently she has developed a more flexible process to meet the needs of contemporary designers, creating pieces that are more versatile to wear and are quicker and easier to make. Helen has designed a series of smaller patterns: some hang like jeweled pendants from beaded strands of variable length, while others fold over to form immensely popular pouches.

Her vision has become more dynamic. In her neckpieces, dangles now swing from various levels. By using a horizontal warp—another innovation (shown at right)—she can create even more fluid contours, which impart rhythm to her more formal designs and outline swirling pools of color in her freeform pieces. Presently, Helen chooses from a wider range of fibers—silk, wool, cotton, linen, acrylic, metallic—with an eye for sensuous textures and luminous hues. She has expanded her search for unusual beads and components—glass, metal, stone, ceramic, organic materials—whose shape, size, or color make them visually refreshing. She even sometimes creates elements in polymer clay to meet her new aesthetic. These focal pieces range from elegant to whimsical, but in Helen's work, they are always imbued with symbolism.

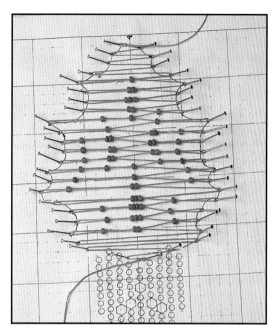

Left:
Pattern set up for weaving on horizontal warp. After the pins are inserted at the outer sides, the warp starts at the top, moving from side to side, then ending at the lower edge. The beads are inserted on the warps before the weaving begins.

Below:
Sacred Lotus Blossom— Horizontal Warp.

Above:
Mexican Cat Pouch: *The narrow black line of thread draws attention to the metallic cat face in the center.*

Right:
Shaman's Spirit: *African shaman's neckpiece combines polymer clay elements with tiny African clay beads and blue glass beads.*

While she continually experiments with new techniques and fresh designs, Helen's inspiration remains rooted in the richness of the past. Ancient artifacts, tribal adornments, traditional textiles, beads, and amulets—these are the wellsprings of her creativity, which she explores at length in *Fiber & Bead Jewelry: Beautiful Designs to Make & Wear*. Helen claims her greatest mentor has been her husband and life companion, Daniel, who nurtured her natural curiosity and encouraged her to delve deeper into the cultures they encountered on their extensive travels and sojourns in Europe, Asia, and Central and South America. They share an enthusiasm for ethnic arts and crafts, and together have collected treasures from around the world.

Helen expands on age-old cultural themes in her work, incorporating traditional motifs, materials, and colors into her wearable art in exciting new ways. Her jewelry evokes the art of a culture or period in which she has immersed herself—ancient Egyptian, pre-Colombian, African, Chinese, Native American, even Art Nouveau and Art Deco—and from which she emerges with inspiration for an entire series of pieces. Research and study of the artifacts of diverse cultures drive her reactions to the

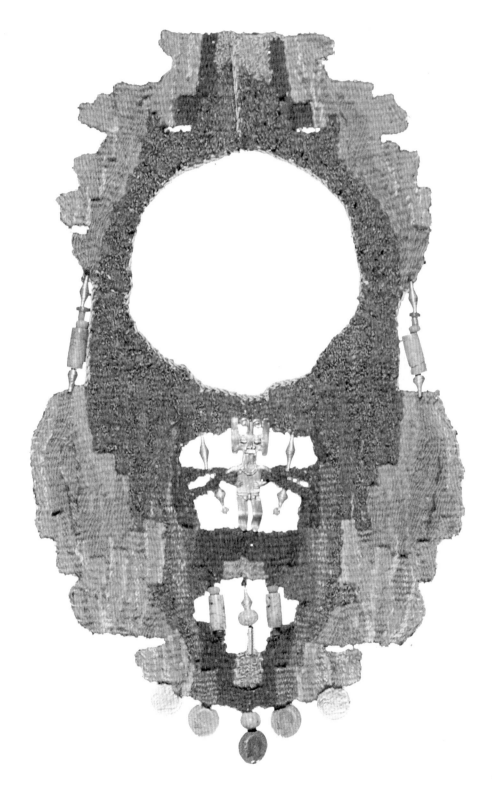

Pre-Colombian Pectoral: *This piece consists of a breastplate woven in two sections. Back and front parts connect at the shoulder with gold and jade elements. Gold replica of a figure and golden-colored coins complete the richly textured adornment.*

13

Above:
Rubaiyat: *Necklace inspired by a gift from my daughter, Ruby.*

———————

Left:
The Way of the Navajo: *This Native American inspiration uses a typical symmetrical Native American design. Notice that the hand-painted Peruvian beads repeat the colors of the weaving.*

power and beauty of their creations, which assume such different forms among different peoples. Rich in symbolism and meaning, Helen's creative responses are true conversation pieces, each with a story to tell through such elemental means of artistic expression as beads and threads.

Beyond the many exquisite pieces she has created, her greatest legacy will be the living legacy of her students, who now number three generations: students who teach new students. Some disciples have sat at Helen's feet for almost two decades and claim they have taken away something new from every session. By generously sharing her skills and sources of inspiration in *Fiber & Bead Jewelry: Beautiful Designs to Make & Wear*, Helen will broaden still further the artistic horizons of many more people and help them satisfy the compelling human need for creativity.

—Joyce Diamanti

Joyce Diamanti is a writer and researcher whose published work reflects her wide-ranging interests in natural science, history, archaeology, and anthropology, especially textiles and beads.

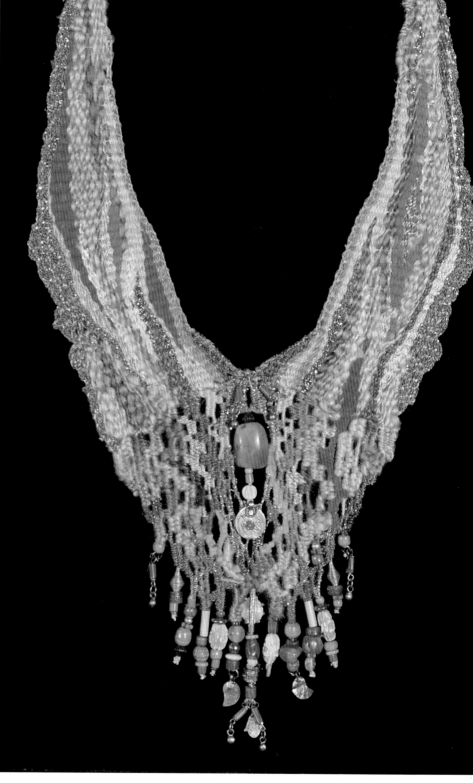

Shalimar: *The delicate colors are associated with the Art Deco style, although the organic shape of the design is influenced by Art Nouveau. The necklace is a freeform flowing design on a horizontal warp, plus bead elements integrated onto vertical warps.*

Preface

As I approach my eightieth birthday, I still remember my mother's complaint that she always had to empty my pockets before doing laundry, as I was constantly picking up stones from the streets of Chicago and the beaches along Lake Michigan.

Now, I can see how that haptic inclination of my childhood led to my fascination with the ancient glass beads I stumbled on in a shop in Israel four decades later. And, eventually to the very core of my artistic identity.

I preferred those old beads in Jerusalem to the fashionable jewelry I found unappealing. These beads felt comfortable to me. They had an appealing visual pattern that had worn away in places and they seemed to have a secret life of their own. I felt connected to that history when I rolled them in my palms, and I thought I sensed the handprints of the people who'd held them before me.

At the age of five, I was introduced to the arts through music lessons, and then at seven took ballet and tap dancing. At eleven, I gravitated to the new artform of interpretive dance. No restrictive, conven-

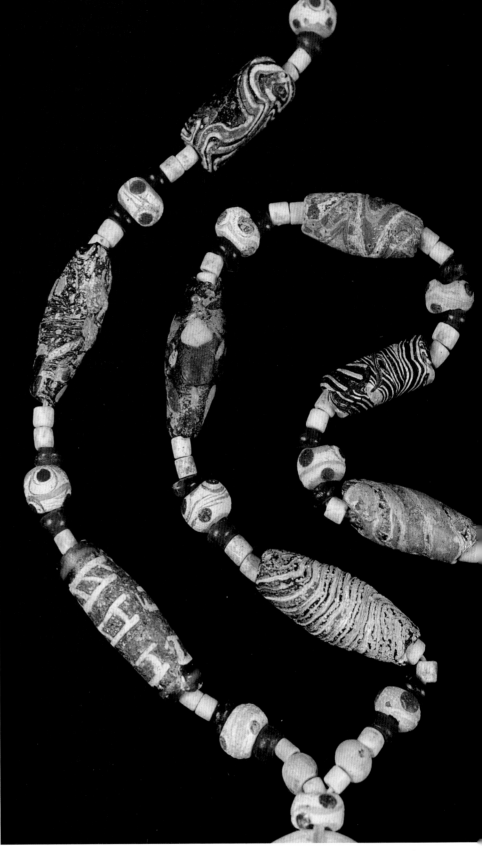

Ancient glass beads (Phoenician, 900 BC) acquired in Jerusalem.

tional tutus or tap shoes for me, but free dancing—barefoot and draped in a loose tunic. For a long time, dancing was my calling and my life.

I started painting during the early '60s. At that time, I was active outside the household doing volunteer work and community children's theatre, but I chafed at the restrictions of suburban life and felt I still hadn't found my calling. Painting became my path to liberation—not so much from my household responsibilities, but more significantly and abidingly, of my artistic consciousness.

At the ripe age of 50, I took my first weaving class, experimenting with off-loom weaving, small-loom tapestry weaving, and soft sculpture, instead of the more conventional, but—to me—tedious, rigid, and monochromatic loom work that dominated in the weaving community at the time. Off-loom, you could weave in any direction you wanted! And, the teacher encouraged us to use color. In this class and subsequent workshops with master teachers, my predilection for spontaneity and improvisation, my lifelong haptic inclination, my impatience with conventional solutions, and my love for color

all merged to lead me in surprising directions.

A strong desire to incorporate objects in my weavings—again, something that was "simply not done" at the time—led me to a breakthrough as I stubbornly followed my own path and, out of an urgent sense of personal necessity, created a technique for structurally integrating beads and threads. Working on a small hand-held loom, which I could carry with me when I traveled, and stringing beads on the warp before I began to fill in the weft with multihued threads, gave me a way to combine several pairs of my artistic loves: not just beads and threads, but color and texture, pattern and freedom, movement and precise detail. I had rarely worn jewelry myself or given much thought to it, but I had been collecting beads, and as my weaving began to be a place where I could showcase them, I soon found myself gravitating toward making wearable woven pieces that featured striking objects, surrounding them in a fully designed artwork.

I'm often asked, "How do you start a new piece?" The feel of a richly textured thread or the sight of a few shimmering

glass beads always triggers new ideas. And sometimes in the back of my mind I connect the bead or thread with a folk motif or exotic treasure from an ancient civilization or a distant place—something I've seen in a museum or have in my own collection.

I usually start with the bead or other perforated object, because it's easier to find threads—which are now available in a wide variety of colors and textures—to go with the beads, than the other way around. I think first of relating the colors of the threads to the beads, complementing them in hue and value, but also providing contrasts to make the beads stand out. I often use some metallic threads, which supply a jewelled look. These pieces, after all, are not rugs or jackets—they're adornments.

Then, I think about creating a fully three-dimensional composition—first with the beads, then filling it out with the threads. Unlike stringing beads in a linear way, my work demands careful attention to what's above, below, and on either side of each bead. Every bead is literally enmeshed in a network of relationships with its neighbors. So each bead's color, texture, shape, and scale have an impact in terms of the vertical, horizontal, and depth dimensions of the piece. And the composition—which includes negative spaces, as well as beads and threads—has to be planned in all those multiple directions.

Also, I "frame" or cap each major bead with minor beads that provide a contrast (especially in terms of shape) to the more important neighbor and separate it from the next major bead. The ending of each strand of beads in a composition is very important to me: it should be well proportioned and graceful, whether the "conclusion" is a small bead, a dangle, or a tassel.

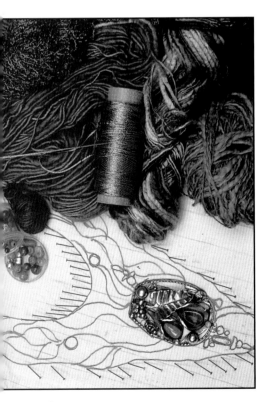

Left:
Mexican Treasure: *When I was commissioned by Stella Krieger of Santa Monica, California, to create a necklace incorporating her Mexican silver pendant with amethyst and jade elements, I had to find a variety of textures and muted colors of lavender and pale green threads to avoid overpowering the delicate colors of the piece.*

Above:
Mexican Treasure: *Necklace completed. Since the pendant is an asymmetrical shape, it was important to create asymmetrical shapes of the colors in the weaving. Additional amethyst, jade, and silver beads were included.*

18

Just as in a symphony, a composer uses a wide variety of notes—short and long, slow and fast, loud and soft—I orchestrate all different kinds of beads and threads, arranging them in patterns of statement, repetition, and contrast.

I have never suffered from artist's block, since I'm usually already planning the next design long before I complete the current piece. And I often have three or four pieces in the works at a time.

The enthusiastic response to the 1993 publication of my first book, *Beads and Threads: A New Technique for Fiber Jewelry* (coauthored with Diane Fitzgerald), has encouraged me to share the new designs featured here. Keeping up with new fashion silhouettes and even new body shapes, my work has changed. I've moved from making larger, more dramatic pieces to smaller, more dynamic ones.

One of my greatest satisfactions has been teaching my ideas and techniques. I probably would not have continued developing new directions in my own creative process without the stimulation of my students, who were excited by the designs we found during our research delving into historic and cultural artifacts. The study of ancient Peruvian textiles, Af-rican adornments, and Egyptian pectorals led us into new visual delights and directions for our own creative work.

I have been immeasurably enriched by the opportunity to associate and collaborate with many artists during my travels, as I've lectured and taught workshops in places ranging from Hawaii and California to New York and my native Chicago. At home, the talented members of the Fiber Gallery in the Torpedo Factory Art Center in Alexandria, Virginia, have supported me in my work for the past twenty-five years and have sustained my creative spirit.

As a teacher and an artist, I have often thought about the Talmudic saying that "it is not your duty to complete the task, but you are not free to desist from it." I see myself as some-one who prizes innovation but also fits into a long, continuing tradition of women weavers and jewelry-makers, both professional and amateur—including my own forebears in Eastern Europe who, out of economic necessity, knitted and wove their own clothing, and my mother, who, though living in easier circumstances, had hands that were never still. For me, fiber work has become a refined but always challenging and exhilarating artform. I invite you to explore its riches.

Safekeeper Pouch:
The most effective contrast is achieved by placing the darkest color next to the lightest color as demonstrated by the black and white areas of weaving and colors of beads. See Desert Rose Pouch Pattern on page 75.

19

Rhythmic Safekeeper Pouches: *The oblong shape is designed to hold a credit card, phone card, hotel key, or money. After completing the front shape, cut a piece of fabric that does not need hemming, such as ultrasuede, and stitch it to the sides and bottom of the woven piece. See Desert Rose Pouch Pattern on page 75.*

L'Harmonie du Monde: 46" x 30" weaving.

chapter one

Discoveries, Inspirations, *and* Evolution

Right:
On a camel in the Old City, Jerusalem,
in search of Bedouin embroideries.

Below:
Irwin Driman's card: dealer in
authentic archaeological artifacts.

Ancient glass beads from archaeologist in Israel.

Beginnings

Traveling in Israel in the late '60s in search of old Bedouin embroideries, I had several unexpected adventures. Among the most exciting was finding a small shop owned by Irwin Driman, a dealer in authentic archaeological artifacts. Rummaging through the fragments of broken pottery and arrowheads from ancient battles in his display cases, I noticed some strands of old glass beads. As I wiped the dusty layers of time from the beads, I was surprised at the shimmering, efflorescent colors and the swirls of pattern on the long tubular beads. On many of the smaller round beads were dark blue circles, like eyes, contrasting brightly with the white powdery background.

As I held this treasure, I suddenly felt connected to the many generations of the past and wondered about the various people who had worn these beautiful necklaces and about how the beads were made, why the necklaces were buried, and how they came to be excavated. This chance discovery marked the beginning of my fascination with old beads, which I started to add to my collection of folk textiles.

I had been painting for several years. During my various long trips in the '60s and '70s (while traveling with my husband as he did consulting work abroad for the World Health Organization and the Pan-American Health Organization), I often became frustrated by the lack of a creative outlet—but I couldn't bring my large canvases and paints with me. When I sat for hours in airports or on airplanes, I needed to do something to keep my hands busy. On one trip, I bought a small ball of perle cotton and a crochet hook in Switzerland. During a flight to the French Riviera, I started to crochet small circles—about two inches in diameter—that could easily fit into my purse. I had no definite plan or purpose for them, but I found that the simple repetitive process was relaxing and almost meditative.

When I returned home and spread out all the crocheted cotton swirls, I suddenly visualized the underwater plants forming whorls

Seafoam Sonata I: *The undulating movement of the crocheted circles imply the movement and rhythm of waves and water.*

———————

at the edge of the beach on the Mediterranean Sea. As I manipulated the circles in the shape of a necklace, I remembered a decorative sea shell among my collection of coral and other sea treasures. That shell became the half-hidden focal point of *Seafoam Sonata I* (shown above).

I started experimenting with ways to integrate these crocheted circles into my weavings. Using a 12" square metal form I had acquired in Denmark as a support, I arranged the variegated colored circles to create a three-dimensional dynamic construction reminiscent of the underwater images I had seen at the beach in France.

Seafoam Sonata II: *Woven square with crocheted waves of perle cotton threads.*

Back at home after many months of travel abroad, I continued to paint large wall pieces inspired by the colorful landscapes and scenery of Israel.

Gradually my paintings began to take a back seat to my tapestry weavings. In my weavings, I continued to pursue my interest in color and nature forms. I had started to incorporate pieces of fabric in my paintings in a collage format. Then I realized that using wrapped threads could help me add an even fuller texture to the surface of my woven designs, which were becoming more and more abstract.

Above:
Memories of Israel:
28" x 32" painting.

Left:
Anemones:
32" x 28" painting.

My preferences in weaving methods began to emerge strongly. Even though I had learned how to dress my table loom with the complicated use of heddles to raise and lower the warp threads, I felt much freer to weave on a simple, portable tapestry frame that allowed for hand-weaving with a needle, instead of a shuttle.

I also wanted more movement in the design and the opportunity to weave on different sections of warp without the restrictions of the table loom, which demands that each entire row be completed before the next row is begun. The tapestry frame had an added advantage —I could take it along whenever I traveled.

October Morn: *36" x 28" weaving.*
Landscapes and scenes from nature still inspired my large tapestries.

Wood Spirit: *36" x 25" weaving.*

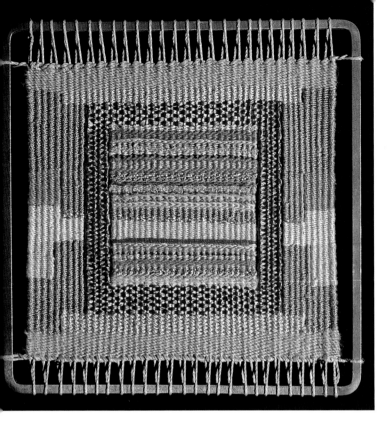

Left:
Homage to the Square:
12" x 12" weaving in a metal frame.

Below:
Homage to the Square:
Necklace woven with Afghani silver dangles.

In preparing an exhibit of my works that included smaller weavings, I decided to make a wearable piece related to one small square tapestry. I thought that would be a way to identify myself as the artist at the opening reception. Besides creating a woven "frame" that enhanced its shape as a necklace, I added some old silver dangles from Afghanistan in an irregular border. To my surprise, a number of people at the opening were more interested in purchasing the necklace than the wall hangings.

One message was clear—wearable art was more collectible than tapestries for the wall. But more importantly, I had enjoyed creating a small, intricately designed weaving that could move with and decorate the body. That very evening I decided to explore the possibility of integrating beads and artifacts with fiber techniques—weaving, wrapping, and braiding.

African Inspirations

In the mid '70s I made another eye-opening discovery, closer to home than Jerusalem, at a small shop called Artifactory in downtown Washington, DC. While I was examining some old Moroccan textiles, a young African man walked in, dragging a dilapidated trunk. When he opened the trunk, I was staggered by the sight of hundreds of long strands of African trade beads.

Although I had acquired a few old glass trade beads several years before in Venice—as my daughter Sally and I wandered along the back canals—this collection had an enormous, dazzling array of shapes, colors, and patterns. It was pure pleasure to behold.

When drawn glass beads were made in 15th-century Murano, Italy, millions of them were traded from Venice to Africa. Some of the long tubular millefiori and mosaic glass beads I found at Artifactory had patterns with molded flower canes in yellow, green, and brown. Deep blue, dark red, and white striped beads contrasted with seven-layered chevron beads. The patterns seemed infinite. From that moment on, collecting old trade beads became my passion. I began to make necklaces that combined the glass beads with bronze elements from the Ivory Coast in a variety of multi-strand necklaces.

Bright Blue Chevrons: *Necklace made with African trade beads (old blue chevron beads originally from Venice) and Kirdi bronze beads.*

Just at this time, I was taking my very first weaving course with Ron Goodman at the Smithsonian. I was so taken with the African trade beads that I made an off-loom weaving using the colors of one of the beads, and then I sewed several of the same beads onto the weaving. Ron objected, pointing out that beads and weavings are two completely different art forms. His opinion was that the weaving should stand on its own. But I loved the colors of the beads, and I had wanted to show the relationship between my weaving and the brilliant beads that had catalyzed it. But I took off two beads, and the next week I took off two more, and finally I took off all the beads.

I continued taking classes with Ron for over ten years, and he became a valued colleague. Eventually he came to agree that beads and threads could coexist. Still, I trace the start of my career as an artist who combines beads and threads to that first, unsuccessful attempt to graft African trade beads *onto* a weaving. I was so determined after that to find a method to incorporate the beads *into* the weaving in a structurally integrated way that eventually I evolved my own technique.

My weaving technique not only allowed me to combine beads and threads structurally, it also gave me a way to bring together my formerly separate interests in textiles, beads,

folk jewelry, and other crafts from traditional societies. When my husband and I spent long periods of time in the Middle East, South America, and Asia, I sought out folk arts and crafts of all kinds. I learned how the designs and color choices, as well as the use of ritual objects or sacred images, express a particular culture's values and beliefs. I could also see how certain formal elements crossed the borders between art forms—how the rhythms of music and dance echoed visually in fabrics, baskets, and ornaments.

When we were at home, I would regularly visit museum and gallery exhibitions of masks, jewelry, and other traditional objects from ancient or geographically distant cultures.

All these discoveries inflected my own artistic choices as I imbedded beads in what seemed to me the most fitting colors and textures of threads, from a cultural, as well as formal, point of view.

During a weaving class I taught, I had given the students—most of whom had lived or traveled overseas—the assignment to bring in something they had collected during their travels that could inspire the class to make a new design. One of my students, Jo Carpenter, who had worked in Zaire, brought in her collection of Kuba cloths made by the Shoowa people.

The richly textured raffia weave of the Kuba cloths was unfamiliar to most of the group. I loved them because of their dramatic design with strong contrasts of black, beige, and rust colors.

I bought some Kuba cloths from Jo. They served as the inspiration to combine African *heishi* beads (slices of ostrich eggshell) with traditional cowrie shells and bronze dangles into wearable art.

This combination provided a setting for the mask I had formed of polymer clay, as a creative response to the mask style of the Lega people of Zaire, which I had seen in an exhibit at the Museum of African Art.

African textiles:
Kuba cloth from
Zaire (Shoowa tribe).
Ostrich egg, heishi
beads made from
eggshell slices, and
cowrie shells.

First I made the mask, and then I made a design that used the colors of the Kuba cloth and simultaneously framed the mask in dramatic ways. For instance, the black area behind the mask supplies a striking background. The rust areas above and below the mask seem like part of the mask itself. They also formally integrate the clay piece into the weaving. I ran warp threads through the mask's ears and added tiny beads to give the face its own little set of earrings. The bronze elements were in the shape of two hands and a banana leaf.

Spirit of Africa:
Woven necklace with old African glass beads, heishi beads, and bronze elements. The African-style mask was made of polymer clay in the style of Lega masks from Zaire. The colors of the weaving are based on the colors of Kuba cloth.

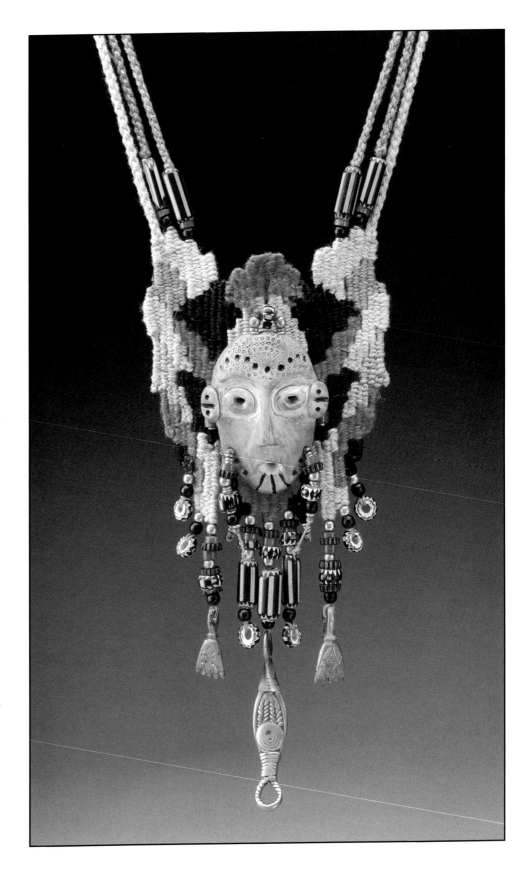

Many more of my necklaces have been inspired by the colors and rhythms of African adornments. In order to create the three-dimensional shape of *African Rhythm* (shown below), I wove the necklace with copper wire as a supplemental warp.

I had been making curved necklaces for a long time and I wanted a change—a shape that would be more dynamic. I also wanted to get more three-dimensional shape into the necklace in a way that was not dependent on beads. The only beads in *African Rhythm* (shown below) are the dangles at the bottom, which add movement. The diagonals create strong dynamic contrasts of color. The sharp movements, rippling forms, and asymmetry of this piece reminded me of the polyrhythms and percussive angularity of African music and dance.

African Rhythm:
Woven necklace in asymmetrical design with supplemental warp of copper wire to create three-dimensional shape.

33

Left:
The Soothsayer:
Necklace started with a bronze Ivory Coast medallion that represents three ancestors and bronze and green glass beads.

Below:
The Soothsayer:
Necklace completed.

Ancestor imagery is important to many African societies. In the Ivory Coast region, wearing jewelry in the image of the ancestor is considered important for protection and as a way of communicating with the deceased ancestors. The tribal soothsayer uses these bronze images to heal and give advice.

The Soothsayer (shown at right) was designed to wear with a coat with African animal images, made by one of my students, fiber artist Mary Preston of Tacoma, Washington. I repeated the rust, black, and white color scheme of the coat—which had black-and-white striped borders—in the necklace. I added green glass beads and bronze dangles to extend the African style and the spirit of the artifact throughout the piece.

Asante gold elements were used repeatedly in this asymmetrical design. Although the thread colors are not typical of traditional African textiles, some contemporary African designs use similar muted tertiary colors. I chose a variegated palette—deep rose, dusty rose, blue violet, hyacinth blue, grape, sandy beige, and nonmetallic gold—in an asymmetrical design of small color areas. The pointed shapes of several of the areas—like the grape-colored triangle on the left side repeated higher up on the right side—create a dynamic push-and-pull effect, tempting the eye to move from one to the next. The gold elements—two tubular gold beads on the lower left side and three tubular gold beads on the upper right side—also create an offbeat rhythm. The long gold piece that hangs slightly off-center resembles wrapped threads and repeats the vertical shape of the neighboring colored threads.

***Asante Gold II:** Asante gold elements in an asymmetrically designed necklace with nontraditional colors.*

I made another African-inspired necklace to wear with a wonderful vest designed by my colleague Ann Curtis. This piece featured silver elements from the Tuareg people of the Niger. The silver Tuareg cross is believed to be a powerful talisman and the five silver dangles, called *tchatchat*, are thought to ensure fertility.

The shape of this necklace was determined by the cut of the vest, which came in close to the sides of the body. I made the necklace long and narrow and designed to be worn higher than my other pieces. The black area in the weaving disappears against a dark background and makes the weaving look like open space. I chose beige to match a color in the vest and added soft blue and black threads. To complete the design, I incorporated old Venetian glass trade beads and heishi beads.

Tuareg Tales: *Necklace features Tuareg silver element from the Niger. The five silver dangles, called tchatchat, are thought by the Tuareg to ensure fertility. The beads are old glass trade beads and heishi beads. The black areas of weaving emphasize the Tuareg silver cross incorporated as the focal point of the necklace. The shape of the necklace is long and narrow, so it can be worn higher than other necklaces, although the adjustable braided closure makes it possible to change the length. See Tuareg Tales Pattern on page 37.*

Tuareg Tales Pattern

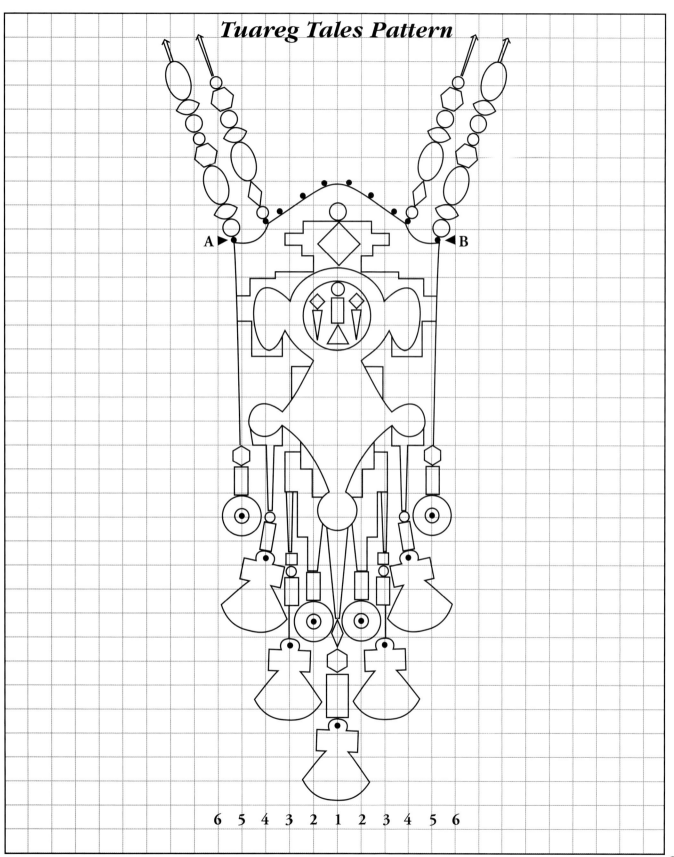

6 5 4 3 2 1 2 3 4 5 6

Ancient Egyptian Visions

Since the discovery of King Tutankhamen's tomb by Howard Carter in 1922, Egyptian-style jewelry has had a continuous appeal in the West. Although it looked beautiful, the primary purpose of Egyptian jewelry was not ornamental, but magical and protective. The jewelry was an amulet worn to ward off evil and used designs—like the scarab—based on cult symbols.

The scarab, or sacred beetle, was placed over the heart of Egyptian mummies and was thought to guarantee immortality to the dead person. We know from tomb drawings that the Egyptians wore pectorals, so their neckpieces became an important model for my work, especially after I saw an impressive exhibition, "The Jewels of the Pharaoh," at the National Gallery in Washington, DC. I was asked to teach a workshop at the Smithsonian using designs and elements inspired by these jewels.

Egyptian Broad Collar:
Tapestry necklace with
gold metallic threads,
faïence tubular beads,
and dyed bone beads.

38

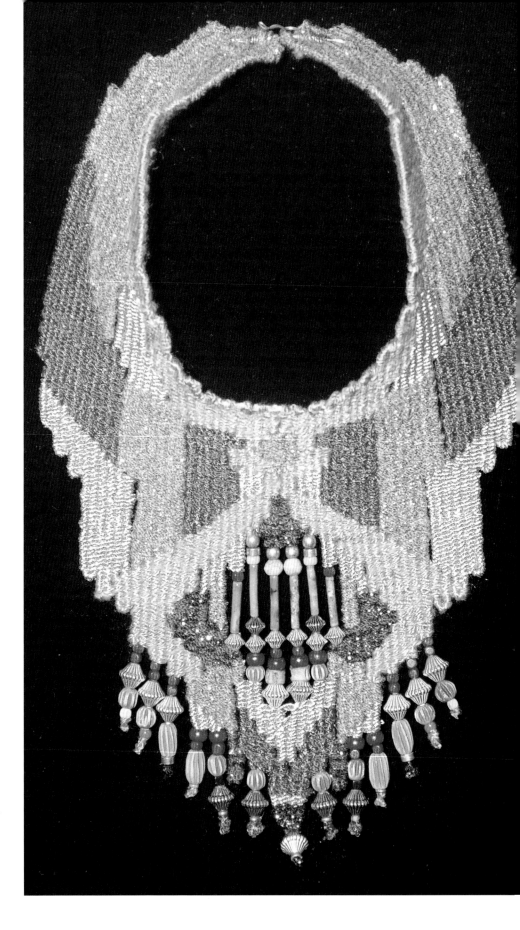

The broad collar worn by the royal family as pictured on tomb drawings appears as an item of dress, as if it were simply made of a piece of undifferentiated fabric. But the depictions on statues and reliefs show more detail: multiple rows of beads and pendants. The preferred colors for ancient Egyptian jewelry were carnelian (the color of blood), green turquoise (the color of vegetation), lapis lazuli (the color of the sky), and gold (the symbol of the sun). The beads were often tubular, made of faïence, or Egyptian paste, which is a form of ceramic made of powdered quartz heated until it fuses and then coated with a colored glaze. My Royal Pectoral pieces were made in the spirit of ancient Egyptian broad collar pectorals and incorporated Egyptian color schemes, although the materials are contemporary.

Egyptian Broad Collar II: *Smaller version tapestry necklace with metallic threads and without beads.*

By creating a mold of a scarab with polymer clay, I could make multiples of the ancient talisman.

Scarab Choker: *Egyptian-inspired choker of turquoise scarabs made of polymer clay.*

One of the polymer clay scarabs was used to create the winged scarab in *Winged Scarab Pectoral* (shown at right); its wings are woven of turquoise thread and the glass and metal beads repeat the favored Egyptian colors carnelian, turquoise, and lapis lazuli. *Winged Scarab Pectoral II* (shown on page 41) is a smaller piece, more delicate and suitable for a queen. It has a lavender scarab and above it—in the weaving itself—I created another talisman, the Eye of Horus, which for the ancient Egyptians would have provided additional protection.

Winged Scarab Pectoral: *Tapestry necklace with polymer clay scarab, plus gold and glass beads.*

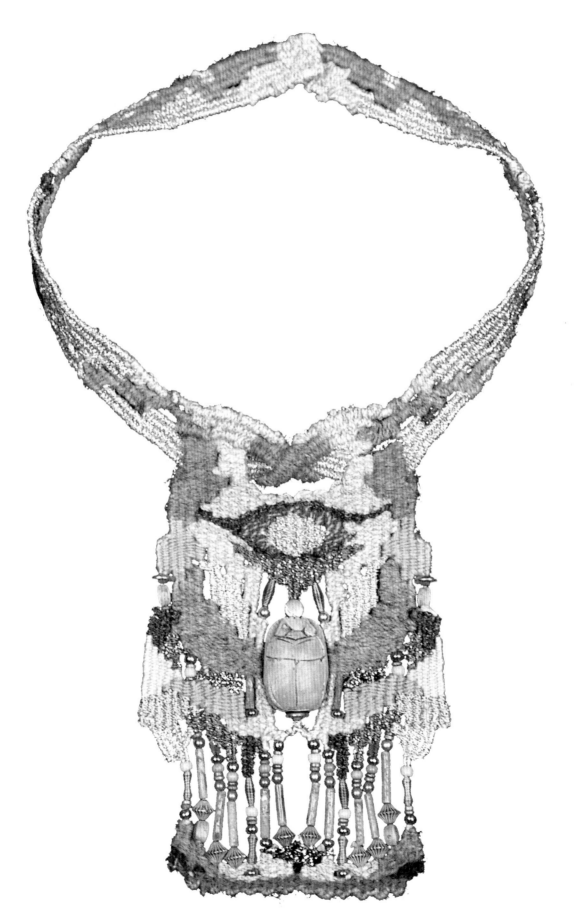

Winged Scarab Pectoral II: *Tapestry necklace with lavender contemporary Egyptian paste scarab and turquoise faïence beads. The center shape represents the protective Eye of Horus.*

Queen Nefertiti's Pectoral (shown at right) is an entirely contemporary piece, but it still refers to the colors and materials, as well as the spirit, of the ancient Egyptian style.

The ancient Egyptians probably would not have worn portraits, but I wanted to include a tribute to Queen Nefertiti, who is depicted on the gold-colored pendant. Her portrait is mounted on a weaving of turquoise thread, with new glass scarab beads and modern pendants.

Queen Nefertiti's Pectoral:

This easy necklace design uses contemporary glass scarab beads from the Czech Republic in the pendant shape and again on the side panels. Since Egyptian royal jewelry incorporated turquoise, lapis lazuli, and gold elements, the colors refer to and evoke, but without imitating, the authentic originals, creating a contemporary feel. Any gold element can be substituted for the image of the queen. See Queen Nefertiti's Pectoral Pattern on page 43.

Queen Nefertiti's Pectoral Pattern

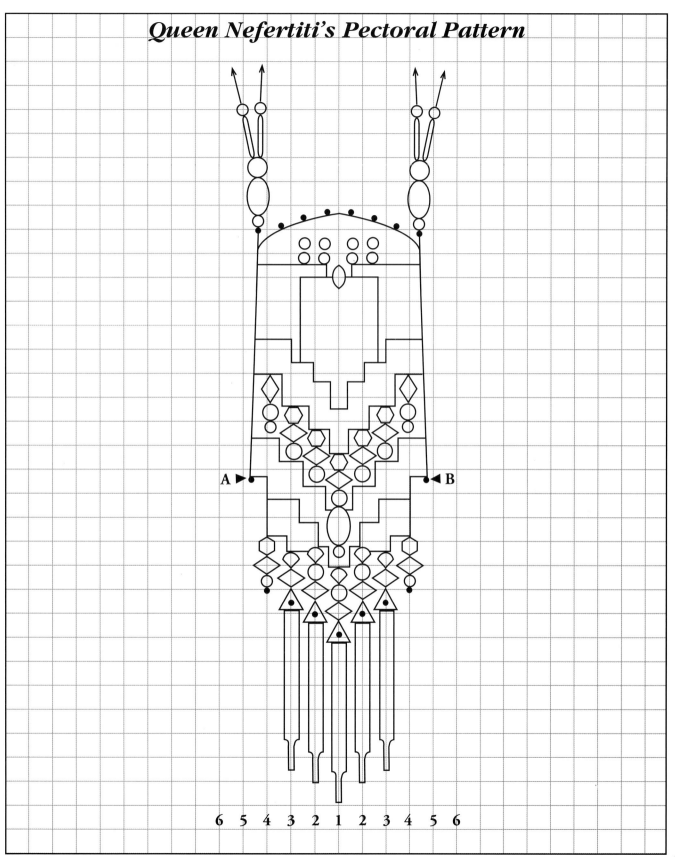

A ▶ ◀ B

6 5 4 3 2 1 2 3 4 5 6

Indian women often wear saris made from fibers in rich, vibrant colors. These ladies, wearing luxurious clothes, sat on the ground while they worked.

India and Beyond

During our visit to India in 1979, I was intrigued by the rich, brilliant colors of the silk saris worn by the Indian women. It was surprising to see ladies wearing such luxurious clothes sitting on the ground.

In Delhi, we were taken by a friend to see women at the cottage industry connected to a theatre make puppets and other theatrical objects. I appreciated the mastery of their craft and the movements of their delicate fingers. One woman worked while her baby slept in her lap.

Left:
Holy man wearing
rudraksha mala
(prayer beads).

———————————

Below:
Rajasthani silver
amulet box
(chhedi ka jantar)
with woven insert.

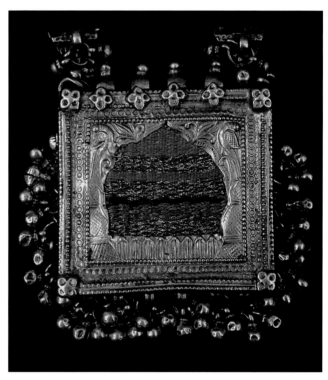

Even the men in India wore interesting adornments. The holy man, dressed in saffron-colored clothing, wears a *rudraksha mala* (prayer beads made of seeds from the Eleao carpur tree). His beard is trimmed so the beads form a perfect frame.

When I bought an exquisitely designed silver amulet box, a *chhedi ka jantar* (shown above) from Rajasthan, the arched opening showed a picture of a goddess on thin paper. I wanted to give the silver box, with its silver dangles and beautiful chain, a richly textured abstract insert, so I wove a miniature tapestry with threads of colored silk and silver for it.

Once I had made that small insert, I went on to make a miniature pendant woven with metallic threads of silver and bright red, with glass beads and small silver coins depicting Hindu gods and goddesses. It is one of the smallest pieces I have ever done, and I have never exhibited it. It remains a private memento of my trip.

India Inspiration:
Miniature 2¹/₂" x 2¹/₂"
woven pendant
with silver metallic
and silk threads
and silver dangles.

For the most part, I created large necklaces with the silver elements I collected in India. These elements included the *Vishnupada* (sacred footsteps) of Vishnu, which are worn as protective amulets.

The centerpiece of *In Vishnu's Footsteps* (shown at right) is the silver elements with the stylized footsteps. The necklace also features dangles enameled with the blue, green, and yellow colors favored by Kangra enamelists, which I repeated in the beads and threads. I made the clasp entirely of silver threads.

In Vishnu's Footsteps:
Large necklace with silver and enamel elements.

Song of India II: Large woven necklace with silver elements from India, including flower-shaped dangles and glass beads.

Song of India II (shown on page 48) features flower-shaped silver elements I had collected in India, combined with pale blue- and coral-colored glass beads, also from India —which is now the world's primary manufacturer of glass beads.

The weft threads in this piece repeat the colors of the beads, while the shape of the whole necklace, and also of the inner peach-colored section, rhymes with the shape of the silver pieces. The necklace has an adjustable closure finished with a braid.

Afghanistan Blues (shown at left) is a large piece that incorporates the colors turquoise, lapis lazuli, and coral, preferred by Afghani artisans, in both the beads and the threads. The tribal elements of warm nickel silver were recycled from old Afghani necklaces, and the coral areas reflect the warmth of the silver and spread it throughout the piece.

Afghanistan Blues: Large pectoral with tribal elements in nickel silver from Afghanistan. Colors of threads: lapis lazuli, turquoise, and coral.

Chinese and Nepalese Influences

When my husband was invited to visit government laboratories in China in 1979, I went along for the trip. The first thing I noticed was that all the adults wore the same clothing—the official Chairman Mao uniform in blue or dark gray. That austere clothing was deliberately drab and made no social distinctions, in stark contrast to the expensive, luxurious silk robes of Imperial China, with colors and images that pictured mythological symbols and had indicated official rank.

Right:

Shanghai Celebration:
Necklace with carved bone beads imitating ivory beads from China. Colors inspired by a blue Ming vase exhibited at the Shanghai Museum. Note the three-dimensional effect at the neckline, created by crocheting.

———

Below:
Mandarin square on silk robe. The flying white crane signifies official rank in the royal court and also symbolizes longevity.

At the Shanghai Museum I was fascinated by the great collection of Ming vases and the intricately carved ivory objects. Later, I called up memories of that trip by making a necklace, combining the carved bone beads I bought at the ivory workshop there with a weaving of Ming blue threads.

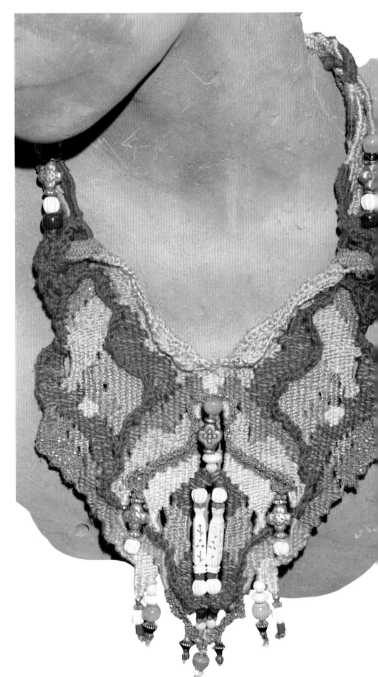

50

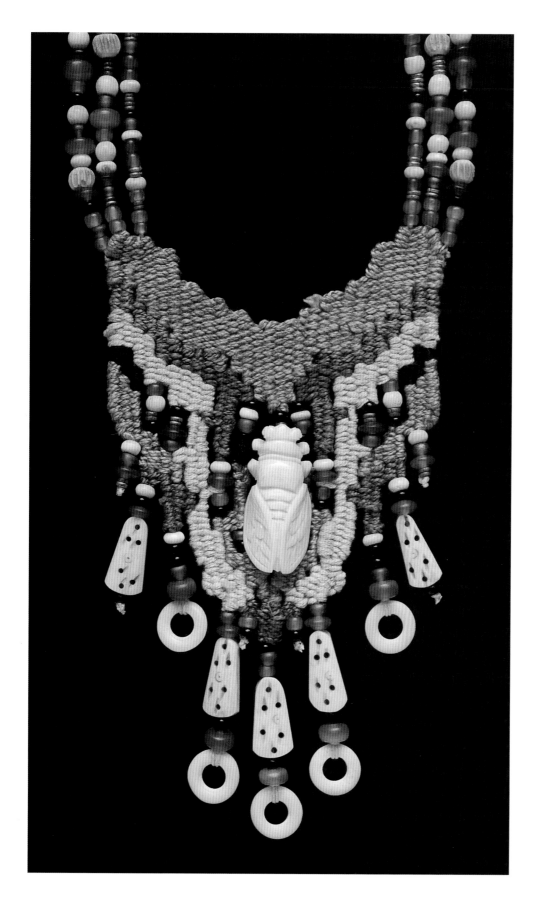

In *Cicada Song* (shown at left), I used more carved bone beads that I found in China. The delicately carved cicada is a model of the insect admired for its "song" —the striking sounds the male of the species makes to attract the female.

In the weaving, the darkest values of thread surround the pale color of the cicada to provide a contrasting frame. The triple strands of supporting beads repeat the colors of the weaving as well as the carved bone beads.

Cicada Song:
Necklace with cicada amulet and carved bone elements.

My woven red pouch necklace combines several elements referring to old Chinese iconography. The silver coin, a symbol of prosperity, is worn both as an amulet and an ornament.

The long strands of carved cinnabar beads are red—the color of joy. The fan-shaped dangles allude to the fans carried by both men and women in Imperial China. The long silk strands at each side of the necklace are embellished with a coral and a jade bead—both considered precious, auspicious, and protective.

Mandarin Pouch:
Woven pouch based on the Imperial Chinese style with a Chinese coin, silk tassels, and cinnabar. See Mandarin Pouch Pattern on page 53.

Mandarin Pouch Pattern

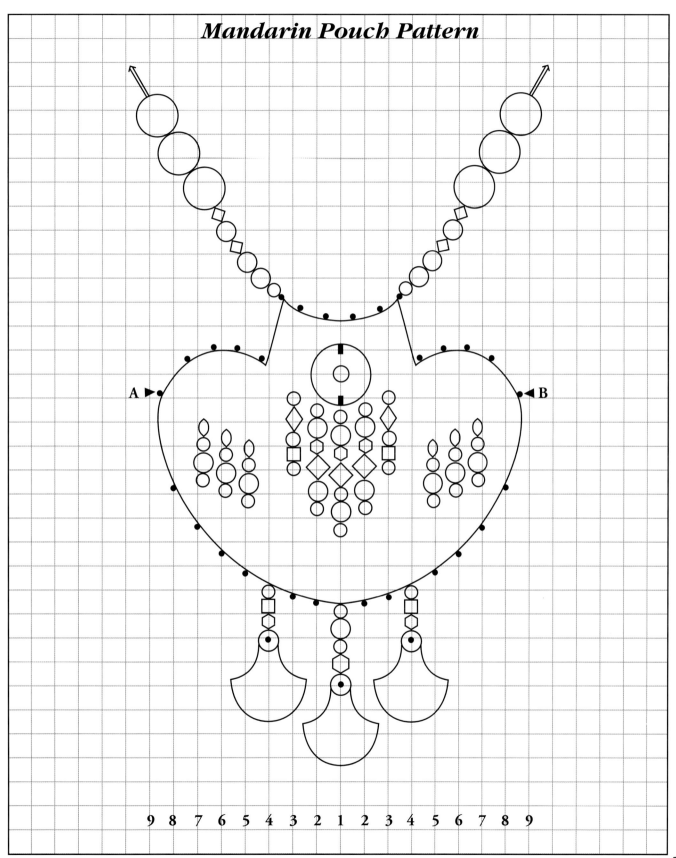

A ▶   ◀ B

9 8 7 6 5 4 3 2 1 2 3 4 5 6 7 8 9

In *Soochow Garden* (shown at right), I pay tribute to the Chinese love for flowers and gardens. Each flower has symbolic significance in Chinese culture. For instance, the chrysanthemum is the emblem of autumn and also denotes joy. The Taoist goddess of flowers is generally depicted accompanied by ladies carrying baskets of flowers.

This necklace, incorporating a silver pendant designed as a basket of flowers with a precious jade bead, was woven on the horizontal warp, which allows for long, flowing lines of color. The closure at the back of the piece is attached to old Chinese buttons, repeating the buttons attached at the lower edge of the necklace.

My Nepali son-in-law, Dawa Sherpa, has taught me about his culture, and I regard the jewelry worn by the women of Nepal with admiration and respect. After I assembled the five strands of coral, turquoise, amber, and silver beads, I realized how important the relation of each bead in the design is to the others. Each one is placed precisely to create a balance of weight and color. The two embellished silver triangles are used to control the space between the strands, while pointing to the wrapped enclosure.

Dawa's Dowry:
Necklace based on typical Nepali multistrand necklace—five strands with beads of silver, amber, turquoise, and coral.

Left:
Soochow Garden: *Large necklace with horizontal warp. The Chinese silver pendant depicts a basket of flowers.*

Peacock's Paradise: Woven necklace designed to showcase a large pin from Nepal with a peacock and a band.

Since the peacock is an emblem of beauty and dignity, I designed a small, delicate shape for the fiber background in *Peacock's Paradise* (shown above), with black threads framing the handsome tail feathers.

The long triple strands of beads allow the small pendant shape to be worn much lower than the rounded collar designs. The gestures of the hand play an important part in Chinese and Nepalese iconography.

The two necklaces based on the sacred lotus blossom demonstrate the different results achieved when weaving on a horizontal or a vertical warp. The necklace on the left is woven on a vertical warp so all the beads can be strung in a straight line, including the long strands at the bottom. The necklace on the right, woven on a horizontal warp, allows the beads to be strung from the side edges. The long strands at the bottom need to be added after the woven area is completed.

Left:
Sacred Lotus Blossom—
Vertical Warp:
Since the flowers are pale and delicate, the colors of the weaving are very close in value.
See Sacred Lotus Blossom—
Vertical Warp Pattern
on page 58.

———————

Right:
Sacred Lotus Blossom—
Horizontal Warp:
This warp arrangement allows for dramatic color contrast through the movement of colored weaving.
See Sacred Lotus Blossom—
Horizontal Warp Pattern
on page 59.

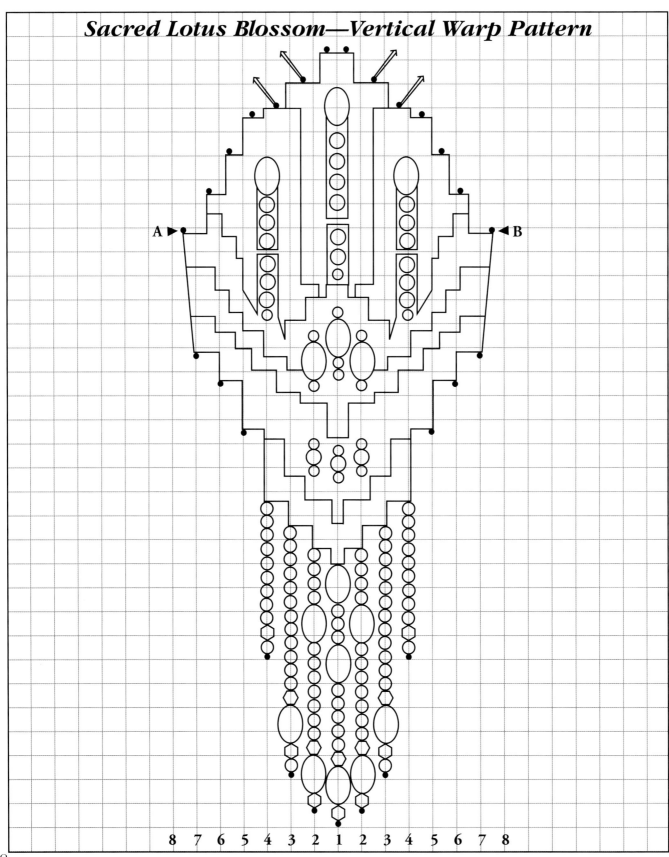

Sacred Lotus Blossom—Vertical Warp Pattern

8 7 6 5 4 3 2 1 2 3 4 5 6 7 8

Sacred Lotus Blossom—Horizontal Warp Pattern

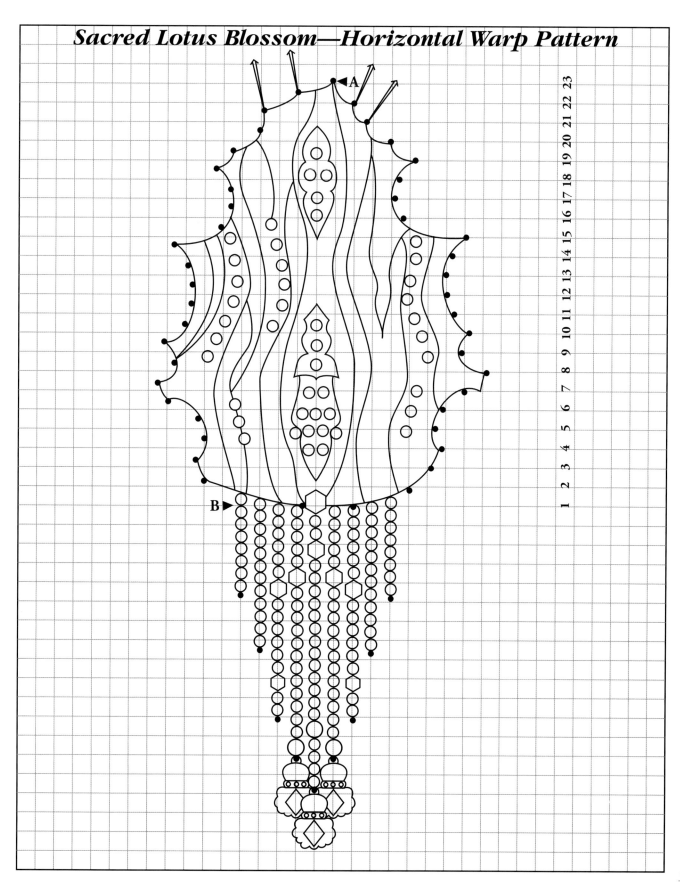

A pair of silver peacocks form a graceful focal point for the large necklace woven on a horizontal warp. This design lets the outer shape undulate in elegant curves.

The movements of the strong, contrasting colors repeat the rounded shapes of the peacock's tail feathers, and the colors of the glass beads relate to the colors of the threads.

Nepali Garden:
Necklace woven on a horizontal warp with a silver pin from Nepal. The double peacock is a popular Nepali design.

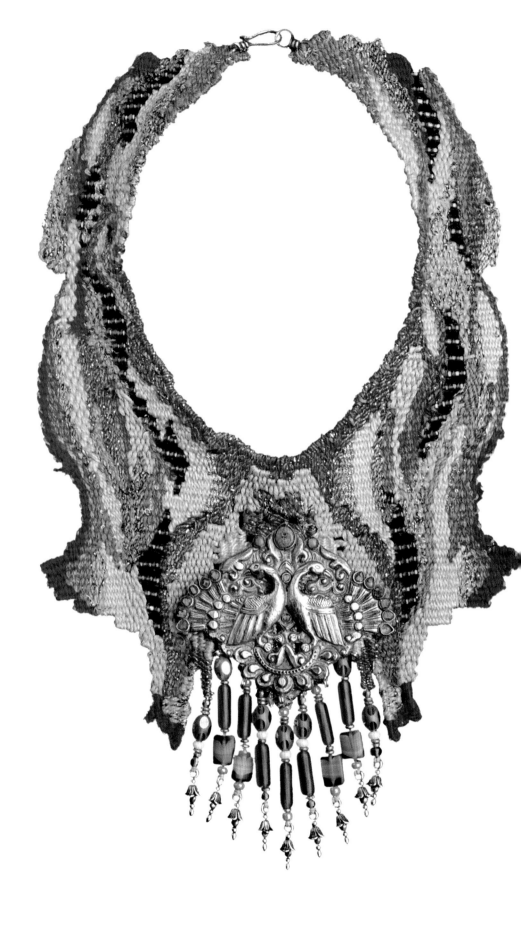

Pre-Colombian and Latin American Influences

During a session of Ron Goodman's advanced group of fiber artists, a visitor came to show a collection of Bolivian Highland weavings. I fell in love with the weavings that day. I had never seen anything like them. The rich red colors of the finely spun yarn alternated with the stripes of bright orange and deep purple of the simply cut garments. Some of the women's shawls, called *mantas*, had wide patterns of fantastic black birds woven against a background of dark red. We gathered around to touch and admire these treasures.

Just a few weeks after that workshop, I was wandering around the side streets of Berkeley, California, and happened on a small store where the owner had just returned from Bolivia. He had an equally discerning eye for beautiful woven goods.

I bought several mantas, ponchos, *ch'uspas* (coca leaf bags), and belts from him. The ch'uspa is a small square pouch made with intricate, tightly woven, warp-faced wool and edged with a narrow tubular braid for decoration and to prevent fraying. The colorful red horses appear to be prancing in two directions. The tasseled pendants hanging from the bottom are punctuated with brightly colored pompons.

Tightly woven bag or ch'uspa from Bolivia. The small 7" pouch is carried by Bolivian men to fill with coca leaves while working in the Andes Mountains.

On the long, narrow two-inch belts, made on a backstrap loom, the popular Bolivian motifs of horses, birds, and flowers are woven in a tight weave with the deep red shades of cochineal-dyed wool. I often wear these wonderful belts with their long flowing tassels and colorful pompons.

I bought replicas of three Peruvian burial dolls, wrapped in fragments of very old textiles—gauze and tightly woven tapestries—from another collector in Washington. Their cloth-covered heads are embroidered with bright wool yarn features, while their arms are made of short wool-wrapped sticks.

The Peruvian weavings exhibited at the Dumbarton Oaks Museum and the Textile Museum in Washington, DC, inspired a course I taught on the body adornments of the Incan, Mayan, and Aztecan cultures. My students and I visited the museums and then created original designs inspired by the textiles and the jewelry.

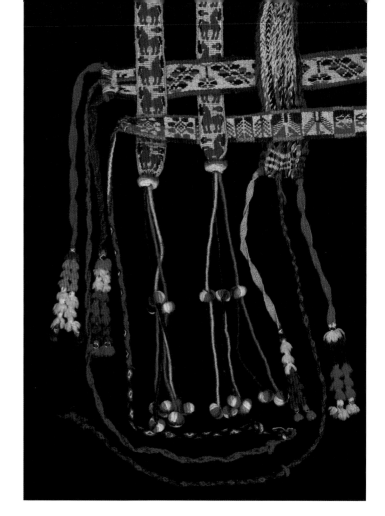

Above:
Bolivian belts woven on backstrap looms and decorated with braids and tassels.

Left:
Replicas of burial dolls from Peru. The dolls have been wrapped in ancient weavings.

At a bead bazaar in Los Angeles, I was intrigued by some unusual objects made of perforated shells, which were identified as ancient Peruvian buttons. I kept them for many years before designing a necklace to feature them.

Paracas Pectoral (shown at left) has geometric hook-shaped magenta and jade colored designs. The buttons were strung onto the warp before I began weaving the necklace. The adjustable closure is connected with braids made from added weft threads.

Paracas Pectoral:
Necklace with oblong old shell buttons decorating traditional hook-shaped design in the weaving.

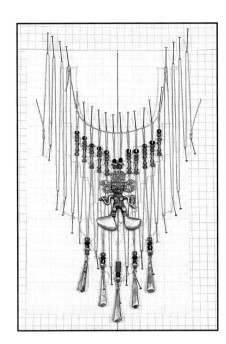

Left:
Orejon Man:
Necklace in progress, using a silver element
with a man's head and animal feet.

Below:
Orejon Man: *Necklace completed.*
The colors are based on a traditional Peruvian textile.
See Orejon Man Pattern on page 65.

The silver pendant figure of a man with *orejon* (big ears) and animal feet became the focal point for a tapestry necklace with colors based on a traditional Peruvian textile. The combination of human and animal features is typical of old Peruvian iconography.

Before the weaving begins on the continuous warp, the pendant, beads, and silver dangles are placed on the warps from the lower edge of the design. The completed necklace shows the stepped geometric design in contrasting colors of gold, green, and dark red. The necklace closure is finished with buttonhole endings connected by a woven tab crowned with two beads.

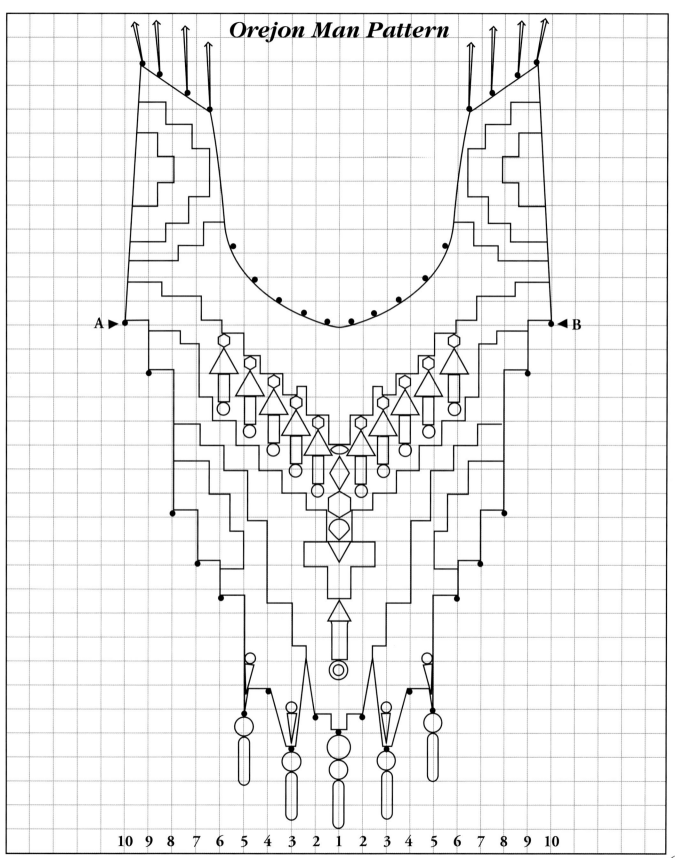

Orejon Man Pattern

A ▶

◀ B

10 9 8 7 6 5 4 3 2 1 2 3 4 5 6 7 8 9 10

During our stays in Central and South America, I came to understand how abundant and omnipresent gold was in pre-Colombian culture.

Gold was not used as money, but was used to make decorations for the home and the body as well as functional objects like vessels. I have been able to buy museum replicas of authentic pre-Colombian gold jewelry at the Metropolitan Museum in New York and the Dumbarton Oaks Museum in Washington.

The focal point of *Colombian Gold II* (shown at right) is a replica of a gold nose piece that also covered the mouth, and the other gold elements and gold threads emphasize the theme of ancient gold.

Colombian Gold II:
Necklace with replica of gold nose piece in a butterfly design.

I spent many hours at museums in Mexico learning about the art of the Aztec people who built the city where Mexico City now stands. And, the local markets were museums of another kind—ablaze with the hot purples, reds, and oranges of textiles, piñatas, and baskets filled with flowers. I realized that the silver pin ornament with the amethyst mask and feathered headdress demanded a setting with the brilliant colors of the Aztec gods' fanciful costumes —a necklace worthy of the ancient Aztec god Quetzalcóatl, the Feathered Serpent. Bright green threads outline the mask's headdress, and long lines of brilliant scarlet move toward the areas of gold and purple weavings. They draw the eye to the mask, which seems to punctuate an explosion of color. The long tubular amethyst beads and shimmering red glass beads are like exclamation points at the bottom.

For Quetzalcóatl: *Necklace based on colorful Aztecan headpieces with contemporary Mexican silver and amethyst pin in the shape of a mask.*

Native American Influences

I am often asked how I choose the colors of my designs. Since my pieces are made to be worn, a particular item of clothing often suggests the basic color scheme. This happened when I bought a beautiful new jacket with Native American designs from the Southwest: the hunchbacked flute player Kokopeli, the frog, the stylized birds, in pale celadon green, a middle-value burnt orange, and a darker raspberry color. I remembered a set of Hohokam shell bracelets I had bought many years before. The Hohokam people were precursors of the Pima and the Papago in the southern desert area of Arizona from around 300 B.C. to 1400 A.D.

The design of *Those Who Disappeared* (shown at left) creates a background of rich colors that set off the pale, off-white, smooth-edged circles of the bracelets, while a woven circle in off-white repeats their shape and color. Although the heishi dangles are from Africa, their shape and color complement the bracelets.

Those Who Disappeared: *Large woven pectoral with old Hohokam shell bracelets from Arizona.*

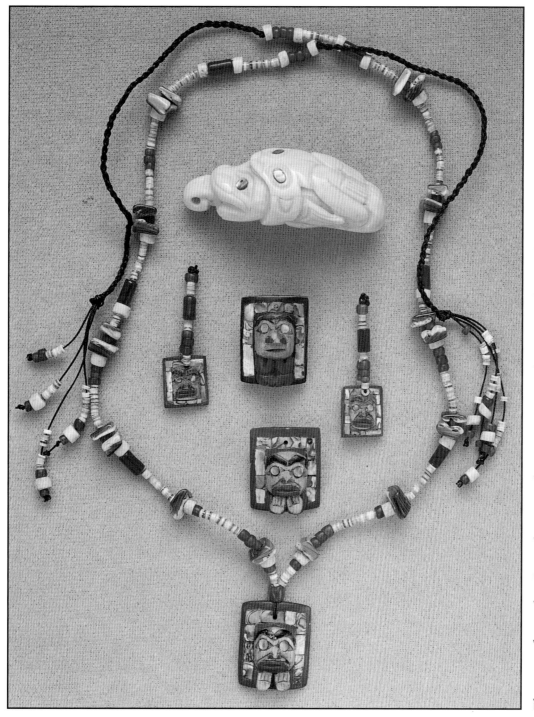

During our annual winter sojourn in Palm Springs, California, I often attend Indian pow-wows, where I especially enjoy the drumming and the dancers with their festive costumes. At one event I met a collector of Northwest Coast Indian art and bought a shaman's amulet of walrus ivory with abalone inlays that reminded me of the Native American art I had seen in Canada. The small carved wooden pieces with inlaid abalone by Lavalle, a Canadian artist, became the focal point of a necklace strung with abalone shell and heishi beads.

The tightly woven Navajo rug weavings with their strong geometric shapes influenced the short necklace *Navajo Spirit II* (shown at right), which is suspended on a double strand of heishi beads. The round, perforated disc pendant provides a strong focal point, while the smooth black and red painted dangles repeat the colors of the threads.

Navajo Spirit II:
Necklace using colors from Navajo rugs with shell disk as centerpiece, heishi beads, turquoise glass, and wood dangles. The traditional colors of the weaving—red, white, and black—are repeated in the colors of the beads and the dangles. The round perforated shell disc could be substituted with any similar shell or large coin. The wooden dangles may be substituted with silver feathers. See Navajo Spirit II Pattern on page 71.

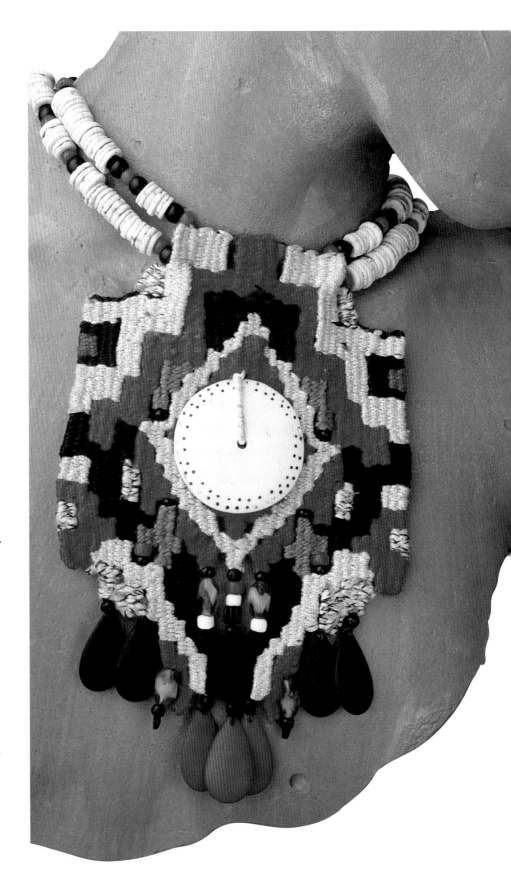

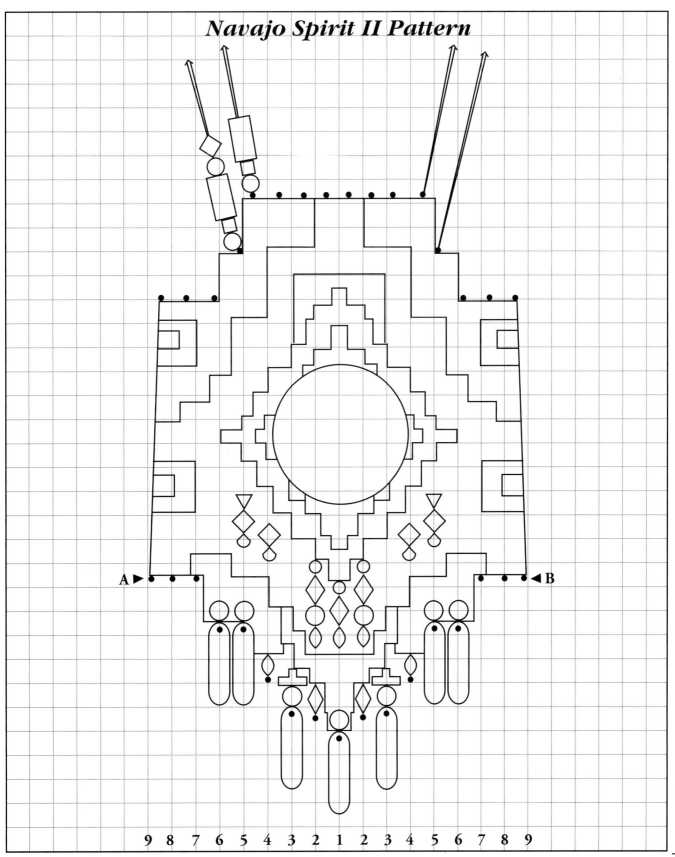

Navajo Spirit II Pattern

A ▶

◀ B

9 8 7 6 5 4 3 2 1 2 3 4 5 6 7 8 9

71

Navajo Spirit III (shown at right) is a much longer necklace. With its hairpipe bone tubular beads and the metal arrow-shaped dangles, it reflects the style worn now at contemporary Native American pow-wows.

Navajo Spirit III: Long necklace with hairpipe bone beads and arrow-shaped dangles.

I was amazed at the masks of the Yup'ik Eskimos of Alaska, which I saw on exhibit at the National Museum of Natural History (part of the Smithsonian Institution). The Yup'ik created the lively, asymmetrical, humorous masks for use in ceremonial dances and storytelling. I was also intrigued by the wide variety of shapes and especially by the appendages of feathers and hands on the faces.

In *Mysterious Mask* (shown at left) I pay tribute to the Yup'ik with my polymer clay mask and the woven background that emphasizes the asymmetry of the mask.

Mysterious Mask:
Necklace incorporating handmade polymer clay mask. Inspired by Yup'ik art of Western Alaska.

73

Desert Rose Pouch: *Small woven pouch with threads of the desert rose color favored by Southwestern Native Americans. See Desert Rose Pouch Pattern on page 75.*

Desert Rose Pouch Pattern

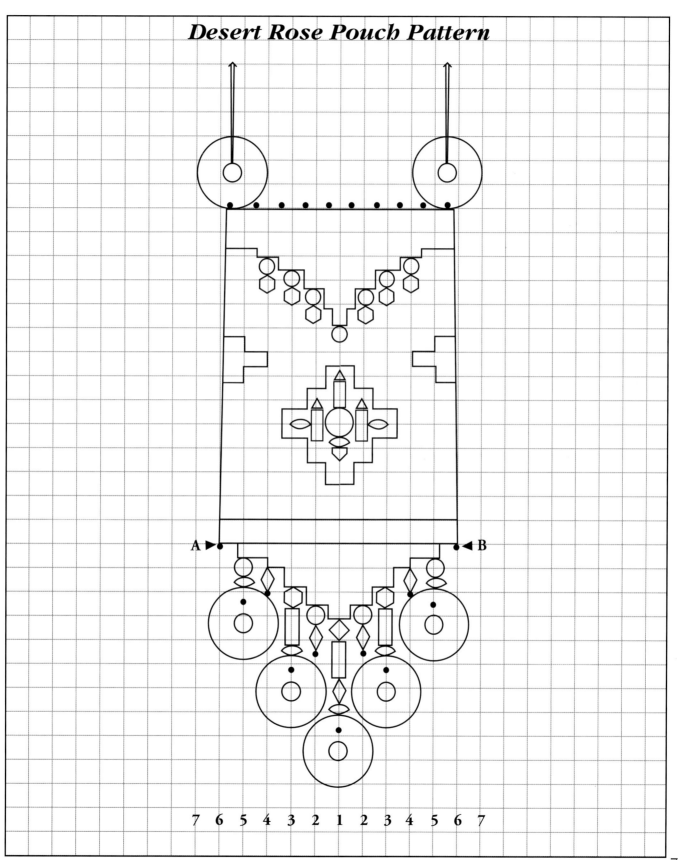

7 6 5 4 3 2 1 2 3 4 5 6 7

Since masks play an important part in Native American ceremonies, I have incorporated many other examples in my pieces. This porcelain mask with a crown of feathers, made by West Coast Native American artist Lillian Pitt, is the focal point of *Stick Spirit* (shown below). The dark purple, dusty lavender, and pale blue colors of the mask determined the colors of the threads. The mask's spirited personality seemed to demand a large, dramatic woven background.

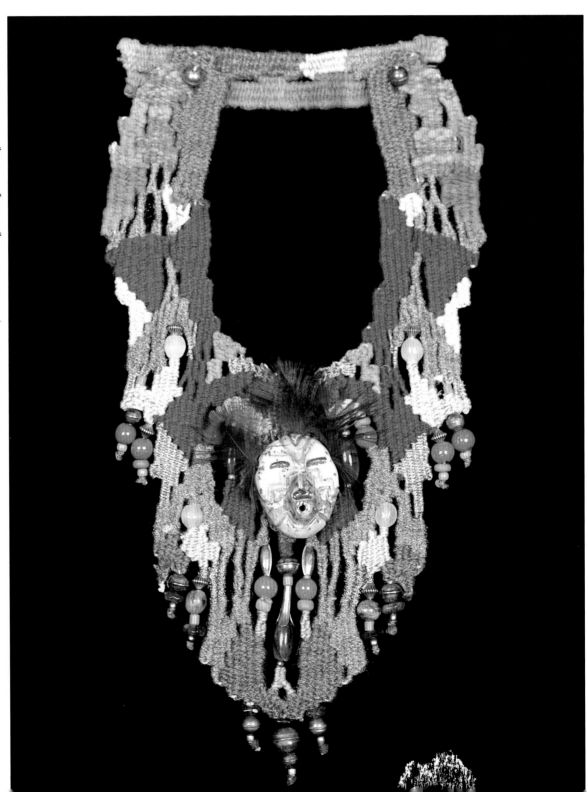

Stick Spirit: *Porcelain mask made by Lillian Pitt, West Coast Native American, used as the focal point of this necklace.*

76

Art Nouveau/ Art Deco

The Art Deco style of decorative arts began to be fashionable internationally in 1925 after an exhibit in Paris. Today, it still sees periodic revivals.

Its emphatic geometric shapes, including triangles, compasses, zigzags, and straight edges—became an important influence on my large wall tapestries.

Echo of Art Deco:
Large 24" x 14"
wall tapestry
based on
Art Deco motifs.

The strong linear rhythms also lent themselves well to the smaller dimensions of my necklaces. During the Art Deco period, creative artisans produced new colors of glass in shades of mauve, acid green, dusty pink, and an orange color called "tango." The pale, grayed colors—raspberry, peach, apricot, lilac, and celadon—associated with the Art Deco style appealed to my palette. Sometimes I have combined Art Deco colors with the organic shapes and textures and the iridescent colors associated with the turn-of-the-century Art Nouveau movement, to create a generalized nostalgic mood for the decorative past without reference to a single period.

Décolleté à la Deco:
Necklace with subtle colors typical of Art Deco in the 1920s.

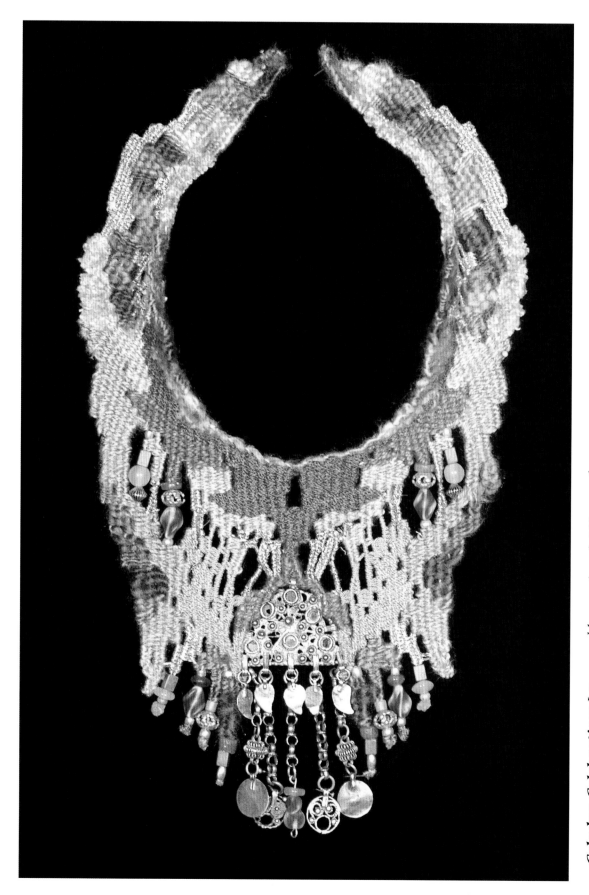

Celadon Celebration: *Large necklace using Art Deco colors: raspberry, celadon, and soft pink with silver dangles.*

Tiffany #4: *Necklace with Tiffany-style glass beads. The pale delicate Art Deco colors of the lavender, peach, and celadon green weaving are repeated in the beads of tubular crystal, iridescent Art Nouveau Tiffany-style bicone beads and faceted peach-colored glass. The many long strands of shimmering beads at the lower edge recall the fringe on the flapper dresses and beaded lampshades of the 1920s. Since the beads are long and narrow, this pattern is designed on graph paper with five squares per inch to allow more beads per inch. See Tiffany #4 Pattern on page 81.*

Tiffany #4 Pattern

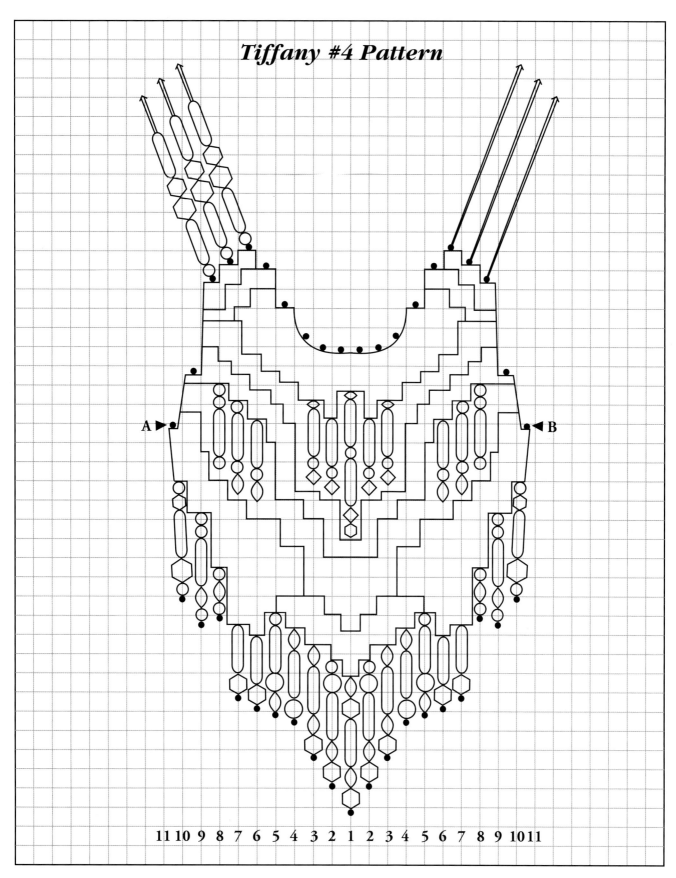

A ▶

◀ B

11 10 9 8 7 6 5 4 3 2 1 2 3 4 5 6 7 8 9 10 11

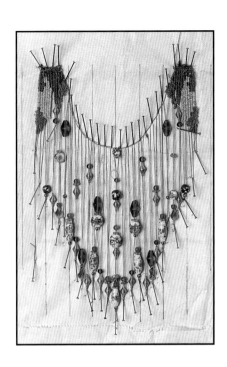

Above:
Bridal Necklace:
Process of stringing beads onto warp before filling woven areas.

Right:
Bridal Necklace:
Pink and white necklace with Venetian decorated glass beads.

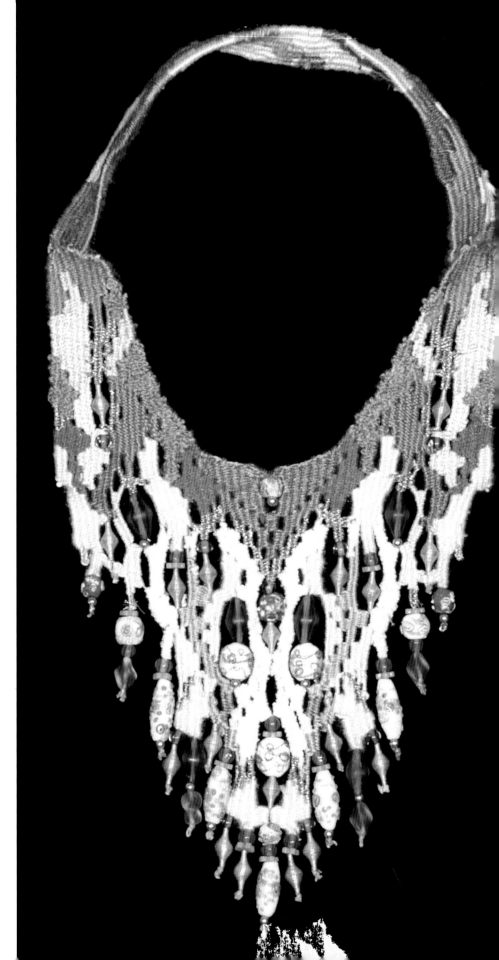

chapter two
the Elements
of Design
for Wearable Art

Supplies Needed

- **Pattern on graph paper**
  Patterns in this book may be reproduced for personal use only. Patterns may not be sold or used for teaching purposes.

- **Board**
  Double thickness of 8" x 10" foam-core board taped together.

- **Pins**
  Bank pins (superplated 17-gauge steel straight pins) or bead pins.

- **Warp thread**
  Waxed carpet linen, 18-gauge, 2- or 3-ply*; available in a large variety of colors.

  Choose a neutral color or a color related to the weft. All the warp, which forms the structure of the necklace, will be covered by the beads and weaving. Warp may also be used in the side attachments.

  *Note: The 3-ply weight of waxed carpet linen is preferable; however, if the beads have smaller holes it will be necessary to use the 2-ply weight.

- **Weft thread**
  Perle cotton #3 suggested for beginners.

  Use any thread that will fit into the eye of a needle—acrylic, silk, metallic, or mixed fibers. Do not use threads that are lumpy or that have a variable thick and thin texture.

- **Tapestry needles**
  #18 and #20 for weaving.

- **Nylon monofilament**
  #8 or very fine-gauge fishing line.

- **Beater**
  Small fork, metal or wooden. Plastic is not suitable.

- **Beads**
  A variety of shapes and textures, with colors related to the threads. Do not use seed beads or other beads with tiny holes since the beads are strung on a pair of warp threads.

- **Dangles**
  Although not necessary, any element without a bore but with a loop at the top or a coin with a hole in it may be attached at the lower edge to dangle.

- **Clear nail polish**
  Use nail polish or clear-drying glue to finish knot at lower edge of beads. No knot is required for ends with dangles attached.

- **Small scissors**
  Use to cut threads.

Step-by-Step Instructions

1. **Preparing the Shaped Loom**
   Shown on page 85.

   a. Tape pattern to foam-core board.

   b. Insert pins at dots indicated on pattern. Notice that the pins at the top of the design are in the middle of the graph paper squares, while the pins at the bottom of the design are at the edges of the squares.

   c. Firmly insert the pins at the top edge at a 45° angle, with the pin head turned away from the design (toward the top of the board).

d. Insert the pins at the lower edge with the pin heads turned away from the design (toward the bottom of the board), thus allowing easy access to working within the design.

e. If you plan to attach dangles or coins at the bottom, allow extra length of warp below the bottom dot, according to the size of the loop or hole of the coin. There will be an even number of pins at the top and an odd number at the bottom.

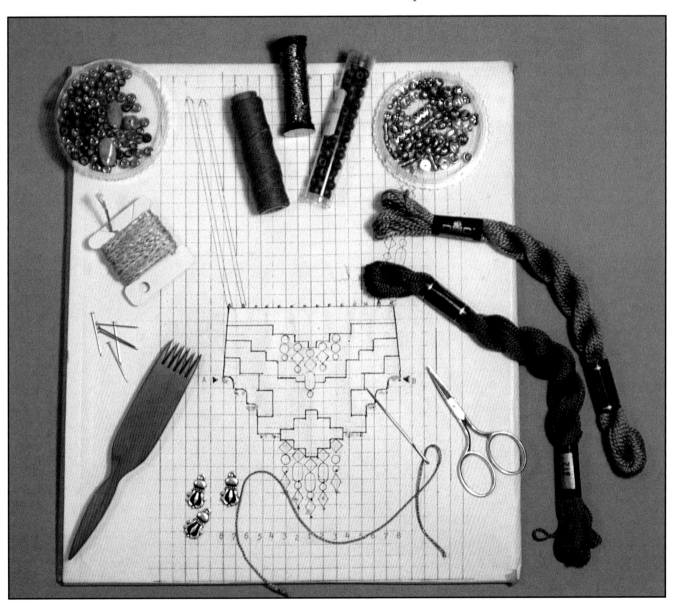

Pattern pinned to board with all necessary supplies.

2. *Preparing the Warp*

Shown below.

a. Anchor the warp thread to the pin marked A (shown in photo below) with a slip knot (shown in Diagram A at right), allowing a 3" tail.

b. Keeping the warp thread taut, string the warp above the pins at the top, then below the pins at the bottom (shown in Diagram B at right).

c. End the warp thread at the pin marked B (shown in photo below) with a slip knot, allowing a 3" tail.

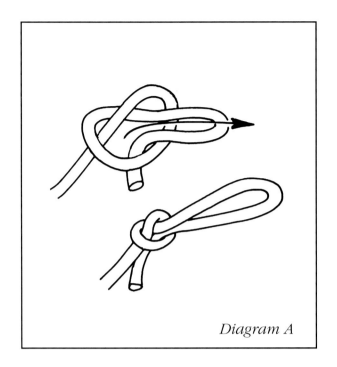

Diagram A

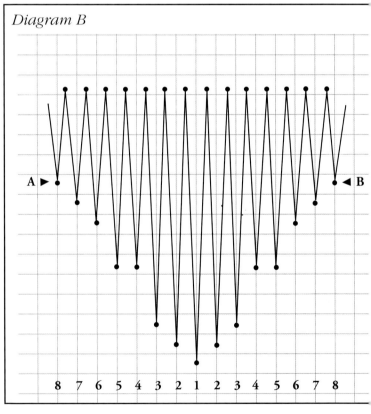

Diagram B

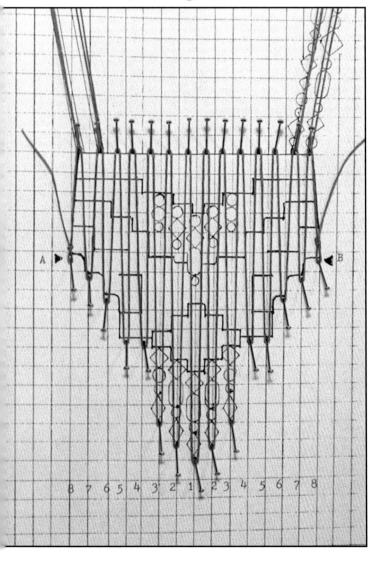

Left:
Preparing the warp.

3. *Adding Beads*

Shown at top right.

a. Remove the pin marked #1 at the bottom of the design, then loop a 3" piece of nylon monofilament between the warp ends and bring the ends of the mono-filament together, using it as a beading needle.

b. Push one bead at a time from the mono-filament up the pair of warps to the place shown on the design. Replace the pin to secure the beads and to hold the tension of the warp. Try to vary the shapes of the beads and avoid using only round beads.

c. Repeat this procedure at adjoining warp ends at the lower edge. The purpose of putting beads on adjacent warps is to create a composition with the beads as a focal point.

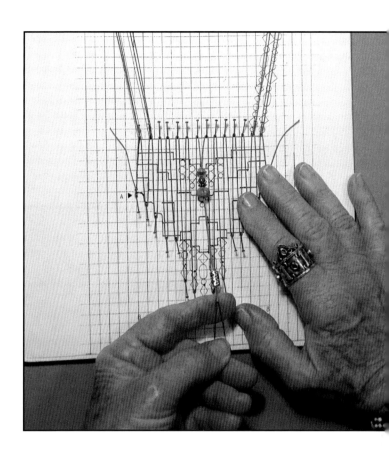

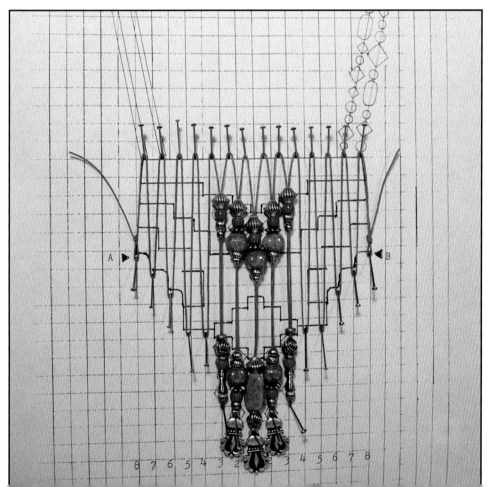

Above:
Adding beads on a pair of warps using nylon monofilament, starting with center pin (#1) at bottom.

_____

Left:
All beads are strung onto the warp before beginning to weave with the weft threads.

4. *Adding Dangles*
Shown at right.

a. Before attaching a coin or similarly shanked element at the lower border, you must first insert all the beads, since the dangle closes the open end of the warp.

b. Remove the pin at the end of the warp and attach the dangle using the "price-tag" or lark's head technique (shown in Diagram C below).

c. Slide the dangle loop up the end of the warp using the nylon monofilament. Push the dangle high enough to spread the loop of warp apart, slipping the element through the widened loop, then pull the element forward to tighten.

d. Replace the pin through the opening of the dangle to secure the beads and to hold the tension of the warp.

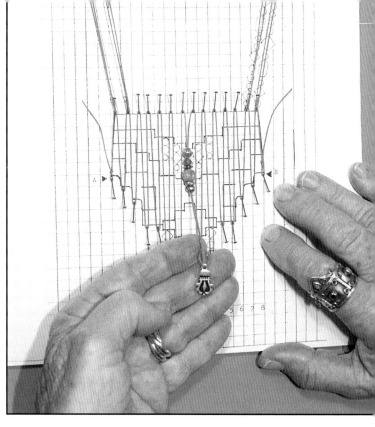

Attaching the dangle with price-tag technique.

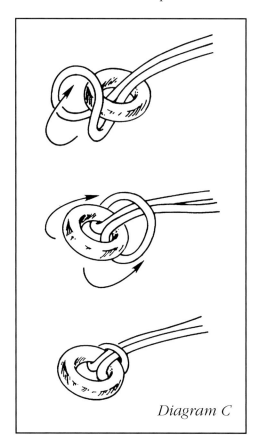

Diagram C

5. *Weaving with a Needle*
Shown on page 89.

a. Begin weaving at the uppermost part of the design with the board top turned toward you.

b. Thread the needle with a single 30" length of weft. A shorter length may be cut for smaller areas of color or texture.

c. Lay the tail end of the thread along the edge warp thread, weaving around it and joining it to the warp as a unit. It is not necessary to make a knot.

d. Begin *under* the first outer warp at the right edge, then *over* the next warp. Continue *under*, then *over*, across the line to be covered.

e. When weaving, each individual warp is woven under or over separately, even though each bead is on a pair of warps.

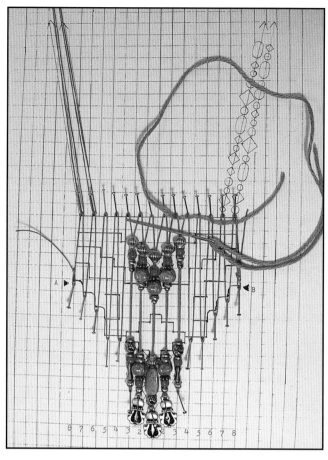

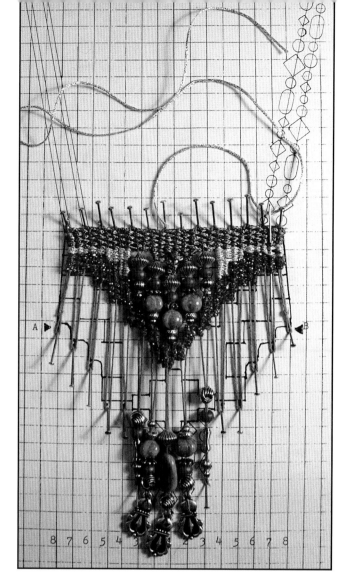

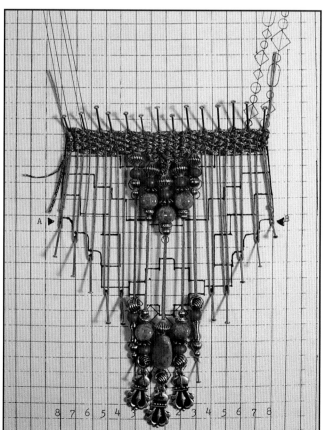

Top Left:
Begin weaving at the uppermost part of the design with the board turned toward you.

———————

Bottom Left:
Filling in first color area.

———————

Above:
Continuing to fill in color areas. Each line in one direction only covers half the warps (since you have woven under half the warps). Therefore, you must weave in two directions in order to establish a solid line of color.

f. Reverse the process in the opposite direction by weaving *under* the warp you went *over* in the previous row.

g. At the end of each row, pack the weft tightly by beating toward the pins at the top with a small fork. Repeat this process each time you weave across one row.

6. **Changing Colors or Adding New Thread**

a. Weave the end of the old thread back through four rows of previous weaving by passing the needle upward along the warp thread.

b. Next, start your needle with the new thread, reversing the way you buried the old thread, by passing the needle downward through four rows of previous weaving. It is not necessary to start or end the thread at the outer edges. You can start a new thread at any point.

c. When your weaving reaches the row level with the slip knot of the warp thread at either side of the piece, pass the weaving thread through the loop of the knot at least twice. This secures the outermost edge of the weaving to the body of the piece.

7. **Completing the Body of the Necklace**

a. In order to secure the beads at the bottom edge of the piece, remove each pin and add a small length of warp thread through the end and tie a knot with the added warp.

b. Apply a drop of glue or clear nail polish before trimming the ends of the knot. Only warp ends with beads require this step. Warp ends with dangles attached do not require further finishing.

8. **Side Attachments: Support for the Woven Necklace**
Shown below.

a. Remove all the top and bottom pins.

b. Loop a 36" length of warp thread (preferably a color related to one of the colors in the weaving) through the top edge where the pin has been removed at the outermost edges of the piece. This will create an 18" double warp length at both sides.

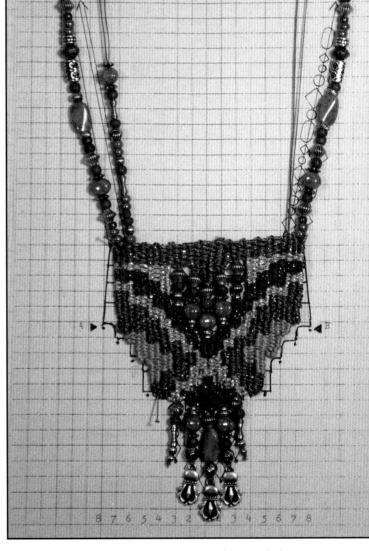

Side supports for the woven pendant. Sliding beads on a pair of warps.

c. If you prefer two strands of beads, repeat this process at the next adjacent pin. This is indicated on each pattern with arrows pointing toward the top of the design.

d. Start stringing beads similar to the combinations used in the body of the piece, pressing the first bead firmly against the edge of the weaving. This creates the effect of a continuous design flow.

e. Continue adding beads to the desired length, depending on the number of beads available.

f. Where the beads end, attach three double strands of weft-colored threads onto the remaining warp using the price-tag technique.

9. ***Adjusting the Length***
    Shown below (left and below).

    a. To provide an adjustable length, which can be tied, make a three- or four-strand braid combining the warp and weft threads.

    b. The ends of the braid can also be pulled through a large-holed bead used as an adjustable slide.

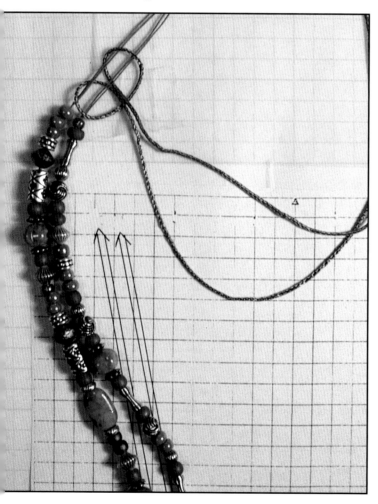

Left and Above:
Attaching strands of weft onto remaining warp to create the braided adjustable tie. By using the same colors of weft for the tie, you can continue related colors to extend the total effect.

91

Beginner's Delight: *This basic design demonstrates the importance of constrasting light and dark shapes to emphasize the pattern. Rhythm is created by the repetition of bead combinations at the lower edge, the center focal point, and then leading to the sides around the neck. See Beginner's Delight Pattern on page 93.*

Beginner's Delight Pattern

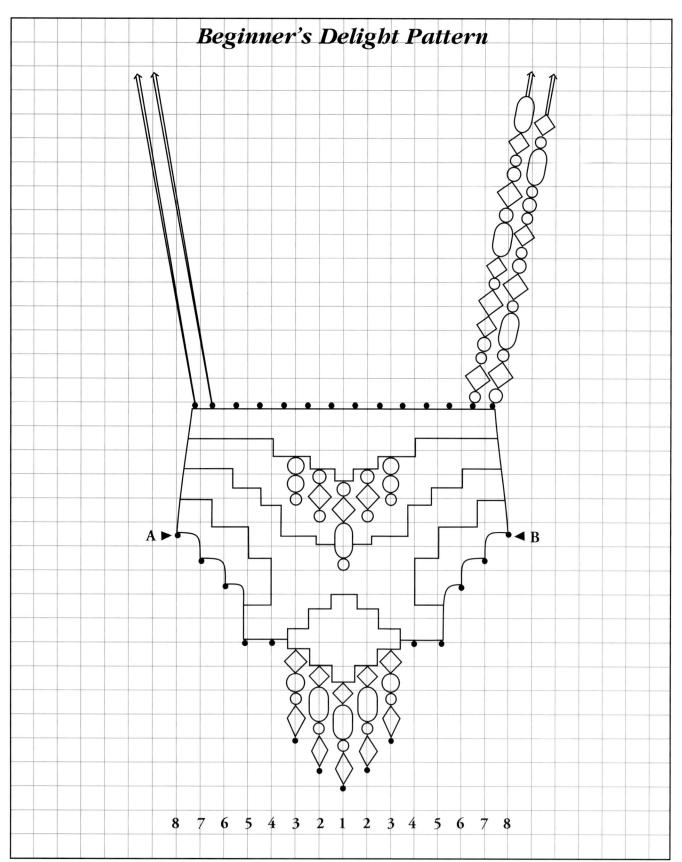

A ▶   ◀ B

8 7 6 5 4 3 2 1 2 3 4 5 6 7 8

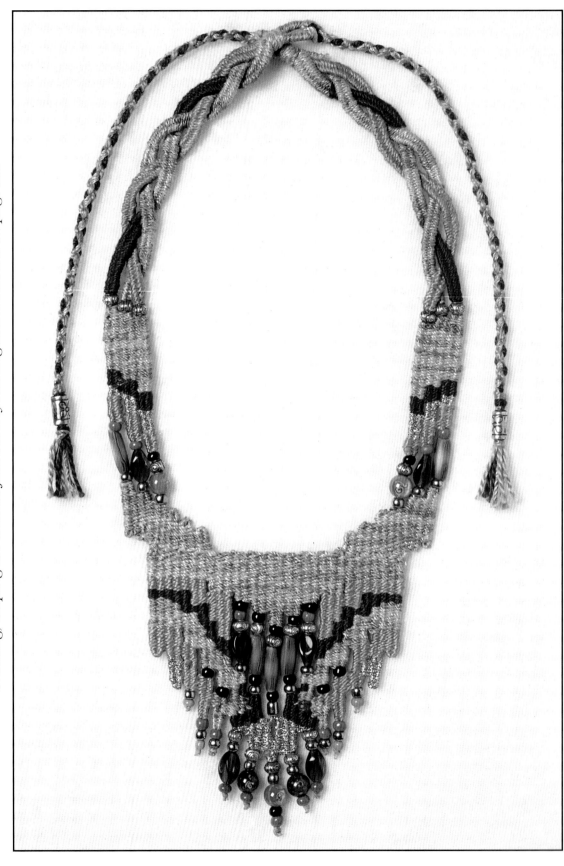

Beyond Beginners: *The extension of warp on both sides provides more needleweaving and beads, which add an important dimension to the shape. The rest of the six lengths of warp are needlewoven in a figure-eight design on each pair of warps. The three strands are then completed by braiding, keeping the strands flat. See Beyond Beginners Pattern on page 95.*

Beyond Beginners Pattern

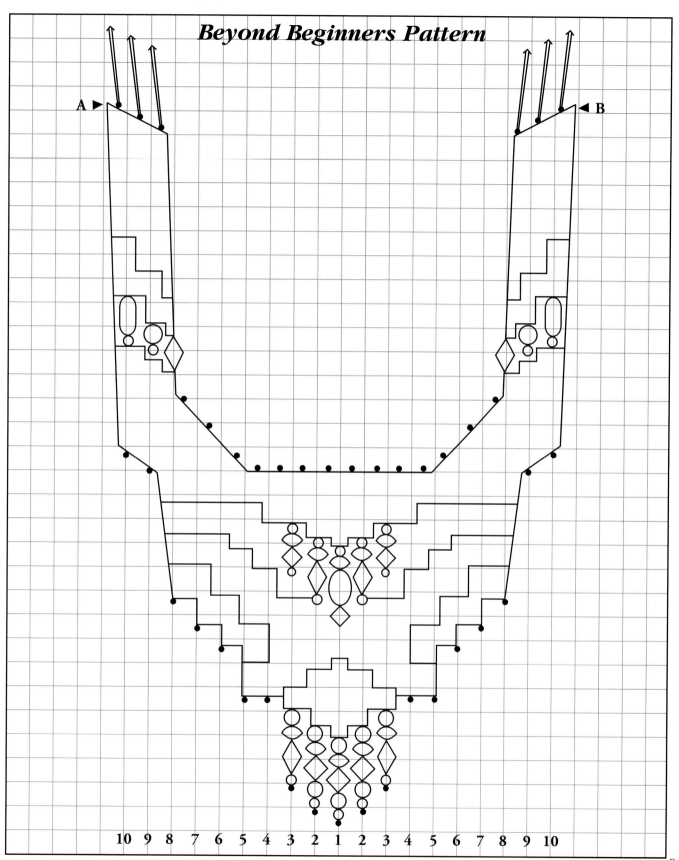

A ► ◄ B

10 9 8 7 6 5 4 3 2 1 2 3 4 5 6 7 8 9 10

Elements of Design

All the art forms—including painting, architecture, and weaving—share basic design elements. But, since jewelry design must be adapted to body proportions, there are special concepts to consider when making wearable art. Patterns have been included as a basis for your designs.

By applying the elements described in this chapter, you can make each piece that you create unique in your own way as you select the colors of the threads, the shapes of the beads, and the special objects you use for the focal points and the dangles.

Scale

The size and shape of all the parts of the necklace should be in proportion to the whole piece.

For a larger necklace, either larger beads or multiple groupings of beads may be used. Large necklaces also require heavier dangles at the lower edge, such as coins or African brass elements. You may use more colors of thread in large necklaces as well.

For a small necklace, use more beads of a delicate scale or long strands of small beads.

Fandango: *This small-scale necklace combines groups of delicate beads, which are repeated at the lower edge and again in the side attachments of the piece, with Art Nouveau shades of silver, gray, and shocking pink. See Fandango Pattern on page 97.*

Fandango Pattern

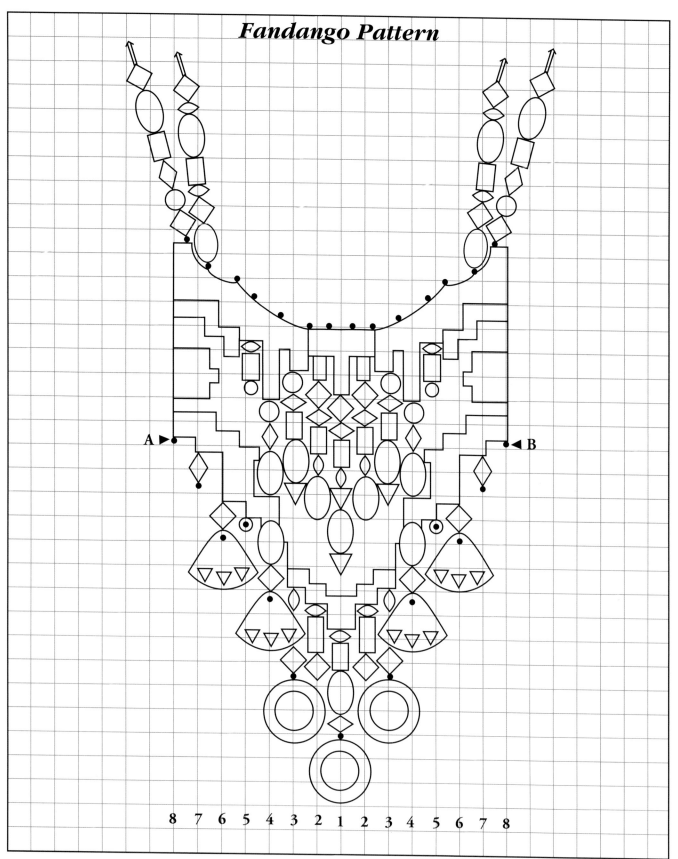

8 7 6 5 4 3 2 1 2 3 4 5 6 7 8

Coral of the Sea: *The large-scale gold coins and large coral glass beads recall treasures of the shimmering blue waters of the Caribbean. These are the elements woven together to form a necklace fit for a mermaid. See Coral of the Sea Pattern on page 99.*

Coral of the Sea Pattern

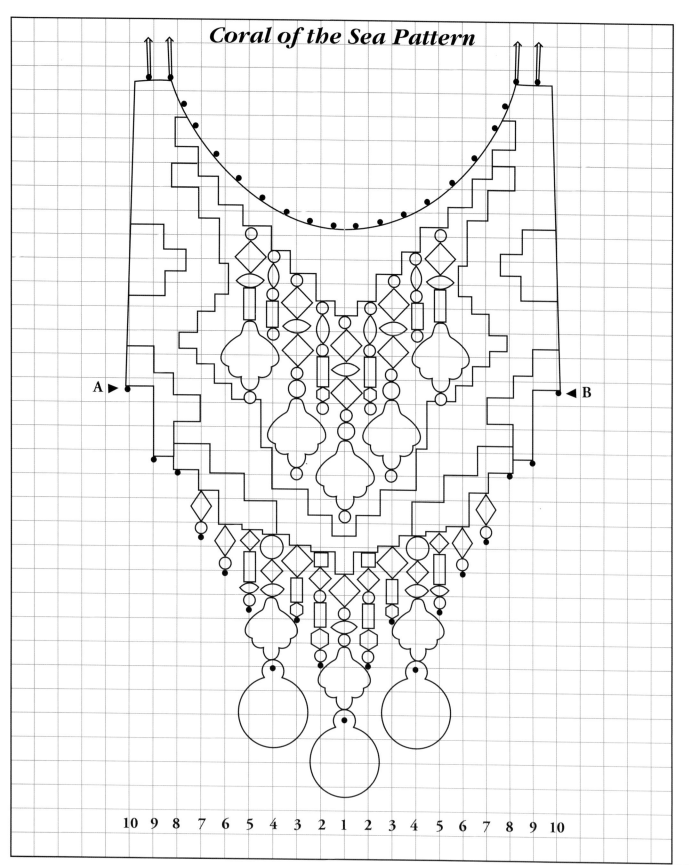

A ▶   ◀ B

10 9 8 7 6 5 4 3 2 1 2 3 4 5 6 7 8 9 10

Hearts of Gold: *The larger scale of this design allows the use of many beads and more color weaving combinations than the smaller patterns. This shape is worn close to the neck, which creates a dramatic effect. See Hearts of Gold Pattern on page 101.*

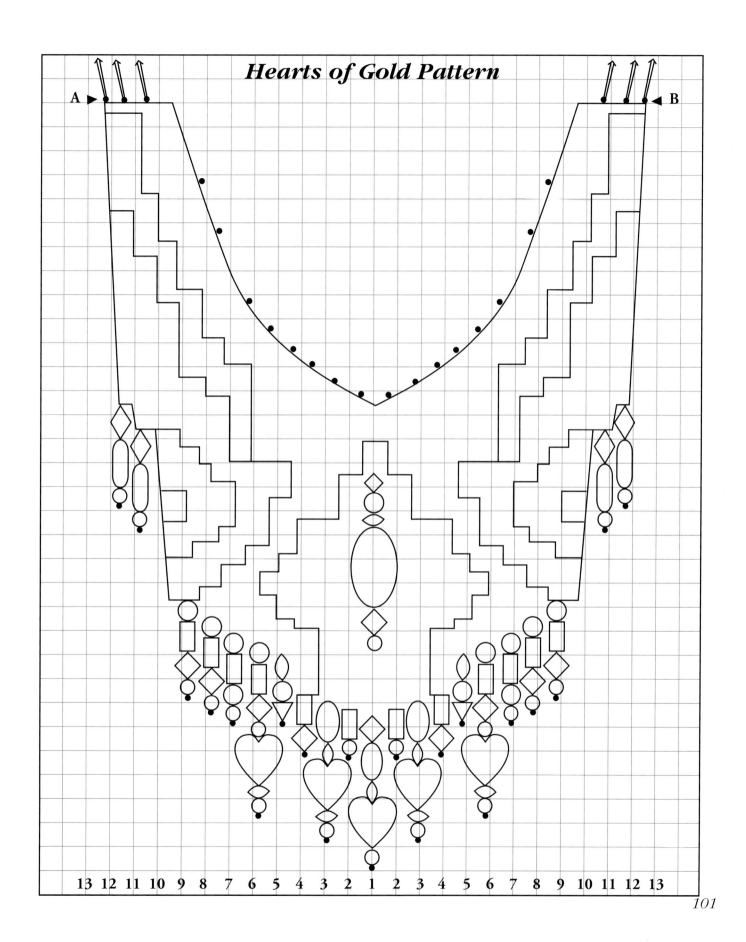

Hearts of Gold Pattern

A ▶

B ◀

13 12 11 10 9 8 7 6 5 4 3 2 1 2 3 4 5 6 7 8 9 10 11 12 13

Balance

Balance refers to the visual weight of a design from side to side and from top to bottom. You can easily achieve balance in a symmetrical design, since both sides are of equal weight visually and physically. In an asymmetrical design, the two sides are not mirror images.

There is a choice between these two aspects of composition: geometric shapes with symmetrically balanced designs or asymmetrical designs that allow the arrangement of beads and freeform shapes of color to flow in an organic way.

The importance of the proper balance between the upper and lower portions of the piece must be taken into consideration when you choose the size and weight of the elements you use. Often a large element used as a focal point in the upper half of the design completely overpowers the lower half of the necklace. The reverse can also be a problem, when most of the heavy beads and dangles are placed in the lower half of the necklace.

A symmetrical design is easier to create than an asymmetrical one, since only one side needs to be composed—and it is then repeated on the other side. Thus, you can complete the necklace design in a shorter time. An asymmetrical design requires continuous analysis to establish the balance and rhythm of beads and areas of color.

Navajo Stripes: *The symmetrical design of Native American inspiration alternates stripes of desert rose and silvery gray weaving. Although I strongly advise against using a dark stripe across most pieces, here the stripes are created within a contained shape. No stripe continues across the entire necklace. See Navajo Stripes Pattern on page 103.*

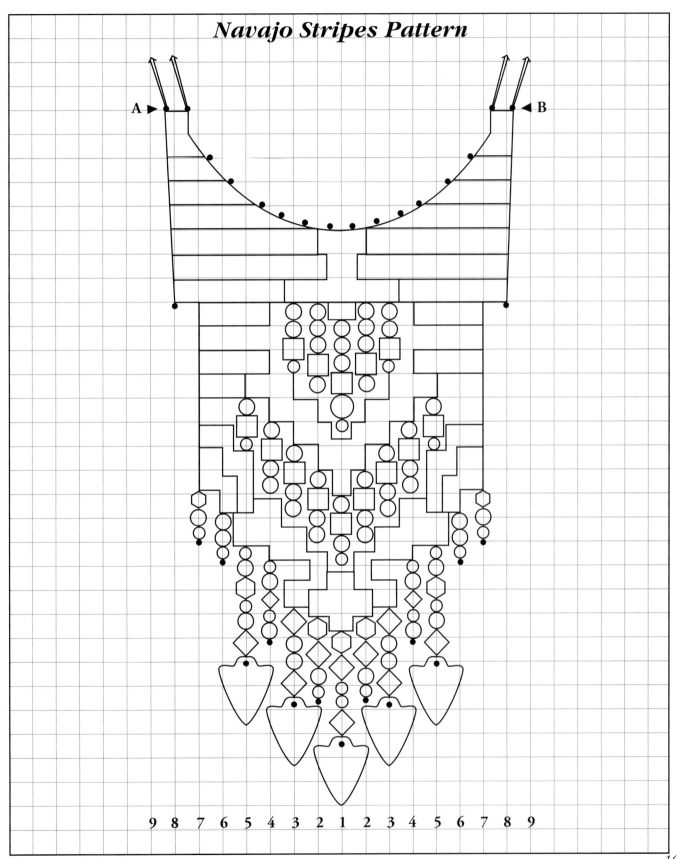

Navajo Stripes Pattern

A ▶   ◀ B

9 8 7 6 5 4 3 2 1 2 3 4 5 6 7 8 9

Indigo Ikat Pectoral: *Necklace in a symmetrical design with indigo threads dyed using Japanese kasuri ikat technique.*

Jigosa Singer: *Necklace in an asymmetrical design displaying areas of color that are irregular. A pin made by Ivan Barnett has been incorporated.*

Rhythm

Rhythm is created by the movement of shapes and colors within the total design. Horizontal lines are static, whereas diagonal lines create dynamic movement. Beads of different shapes create a rhythmic pattern when they are placed diagonally and the pattern is repeated within the shape.

Just as in a musical composition a leitmotif is repeated, so in the design of a necklace the repetition of bead combinations creates a rhythmic structure. Also important is the repetition of areas of color at various levels.

Attaching a silk tassel at the lower edge of a necklace provides an elegant rhythm as the body moves.

In choosing beads, the most important thing to look for is a variety of interesting shapes. Even a round bead can be given a rhythmic quality by placing small beads above and below the center bead, then adding adjacent narrow tubular beads along each side.

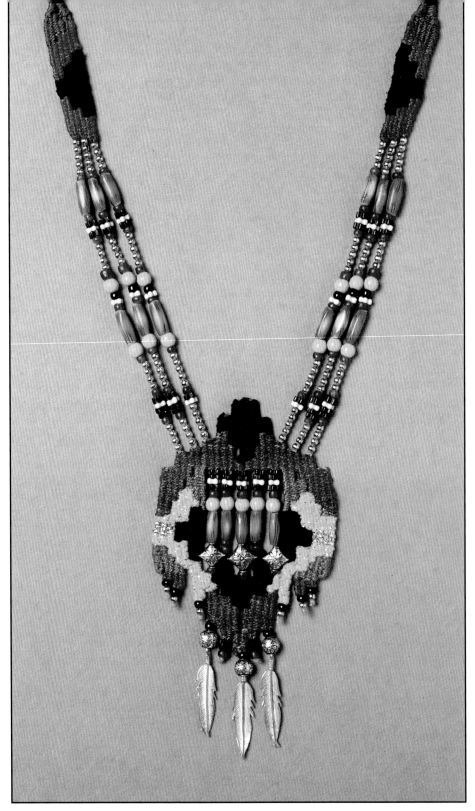

Mexican Vest Motif: *The repetition of bead combinations and thread colors starting from the lower edge to the center and continuing to the upper strands creates a rhythmic structure in this necklace. The bright colors of a Mexican woven vest were the inspiration for this piece. See Mexican Vest Motif Pattern on page 107.*

Mexican Vest Motif Pattern

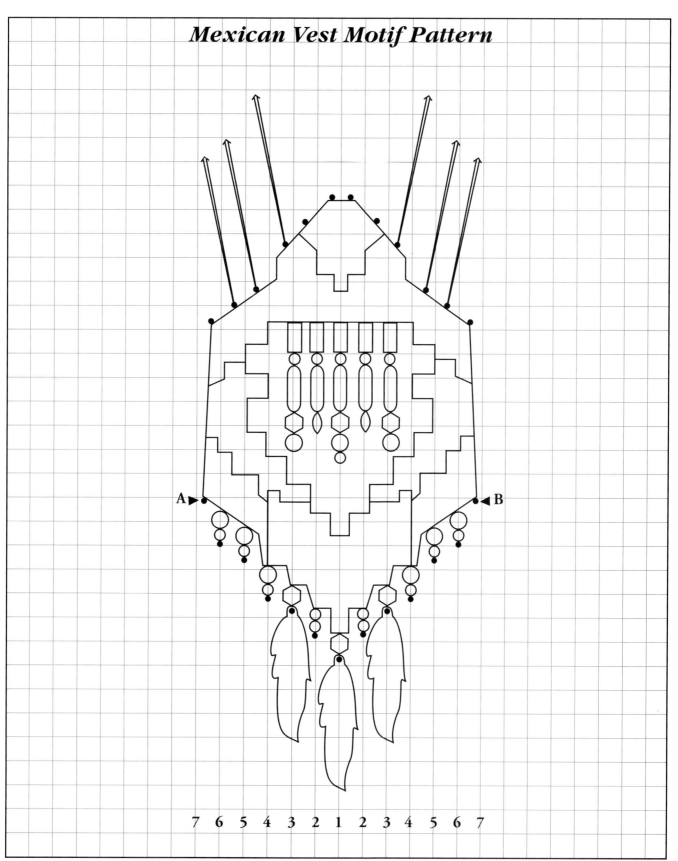

7 6 5 4 3 2 1 2 3 4 5 6 7

Jade Pendants: *The long strands of weaving ending with jade elements and arrow-shaped dangles allow for graceful movement. Although the disc and pendants are made of Chinese jade, any other material may be substituted—bone, metal, ceramic, even polymer clay elements. See Jade Pendants Pattern on page 109.*

Jade Pendants Pattern

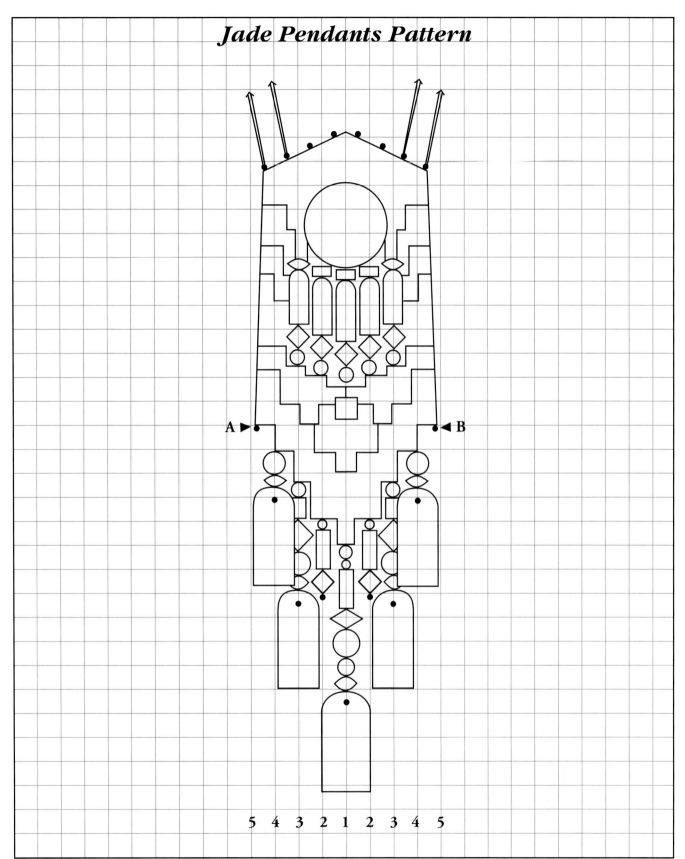

A ▶

B ◀

5 4 3 2 1 2 3 4 5

Kimono Expressions—Horizontal Warp: In contrast to the geometric precision of Kimono Expressions—Vertical Warp on page 113, here the fluid movement of colors evokes images of elegant silk kosode. See Kimono Expressions—Horizontal Warp Pattern on page 111.

Kimono Expressions—Horizontal Warp Pattern

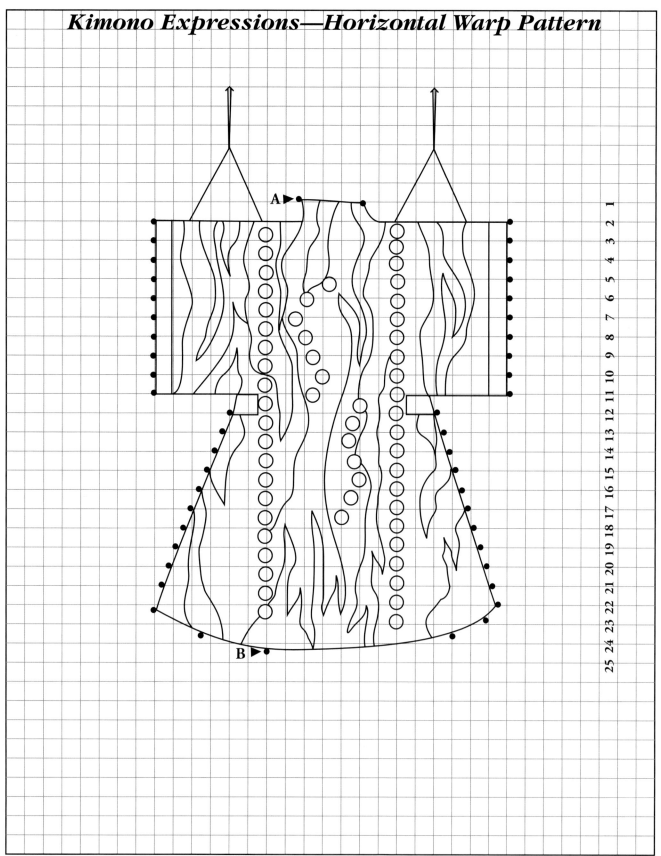

A ▶

B ▶

25 24 23 22 21 20 19 18 17 16 15 14 13 12 11 10 9 8 7 6 5 4 3 2 1

Kimono Expressions—Vertical Warp: *The traditional kimono shape is woven with silk threads. The Tibetan turquoise beads combine with the line of delicate Japanese glass beads for a Pan-Asian fusion effect. See Kimono Expressions—Vertical Warp Pattern on page 113.*

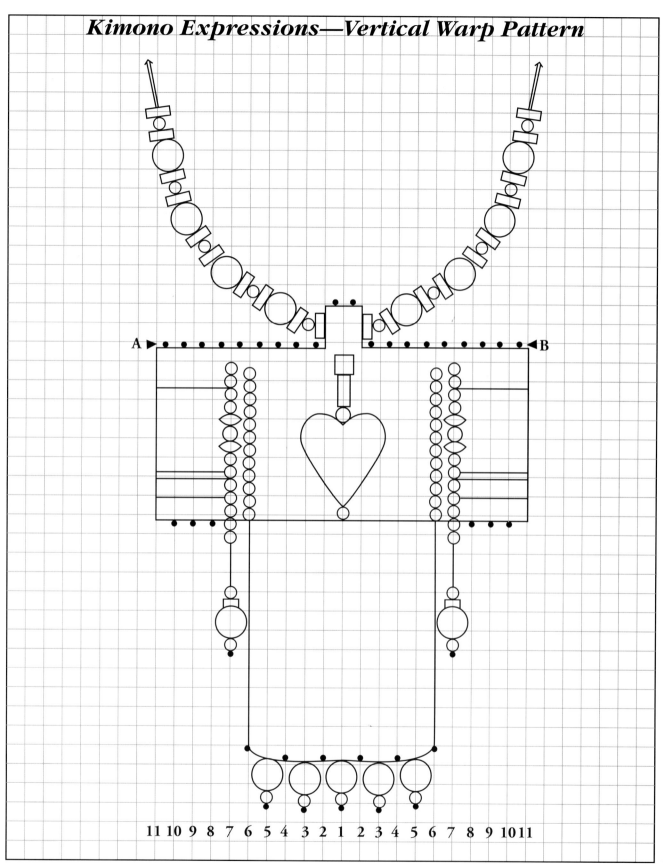

Kimono Expressions—Vertical Warp Pattern

A ▶ ◀ B

11 10 9 8 7 6 5 4 3 2 1 2 3 4 5 6 7 8 9 10 11

Focal Point

The focal point is the primary point of attention that attracts the eye to the piece as a whole. This can be achieved with a group of unique beads at the center of the necklace. A single large object placed at the center of the piece can be an effective focal point or a narrow line of threads framing the center object can draw attention to the focal point.

Dark areas adjacent to any shape add a dramatic dimension.

The focal point can be given more attention by providing strong color contrast, using light-colored threads adjacent to the dark area of beads or dark values adjacent to a light focal group of beads.

Five Little Kittens:
The larger bead
represents the
mother cat, while
the smaller ones
refer to the
kittens who lost
their mittens.
The fine line
of black thread
draws attention
to the center focal point.
See Five Little Kittens
Pattern on page 115.

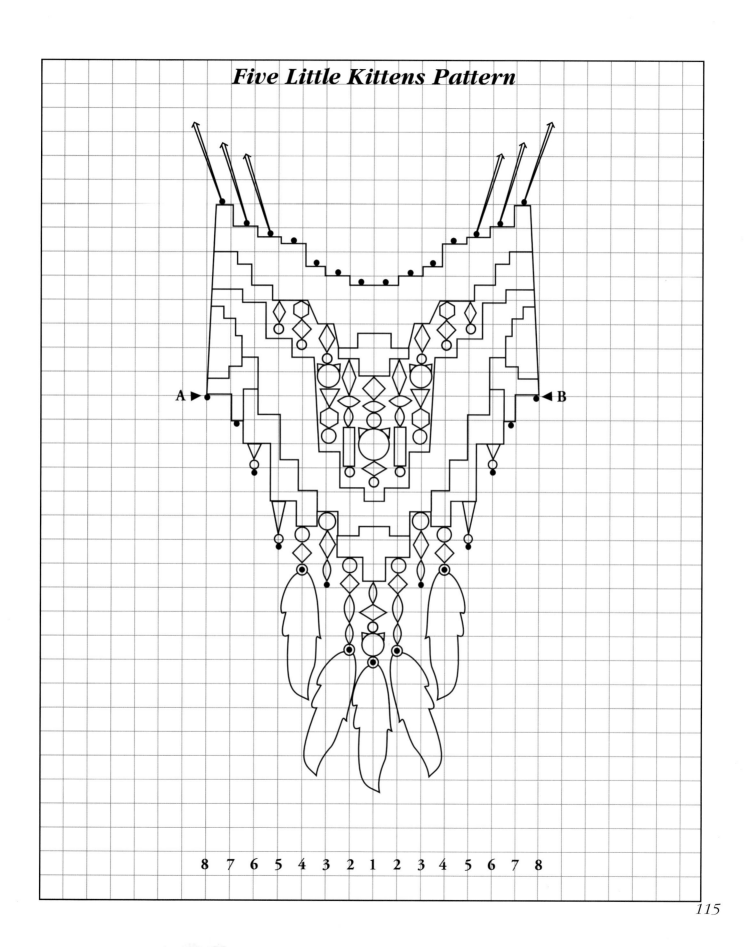

Five Little Kittens Pattern

A ► ◄ B

8 7 6 5 4 3 2 1 2 3 4 5 6 7 8

Homage to Georgia O'Keeffe: *The gift of a carved palm nut pendant representing an animal skull brought to mind Georgia O'Keeffe's famous paintings. The earth tones evoke the New Mexico desert landscape. See Homage to Georgia O'Keeffe Pattern on page 117.*

Homage to Georgia O'Keeffe Pattern

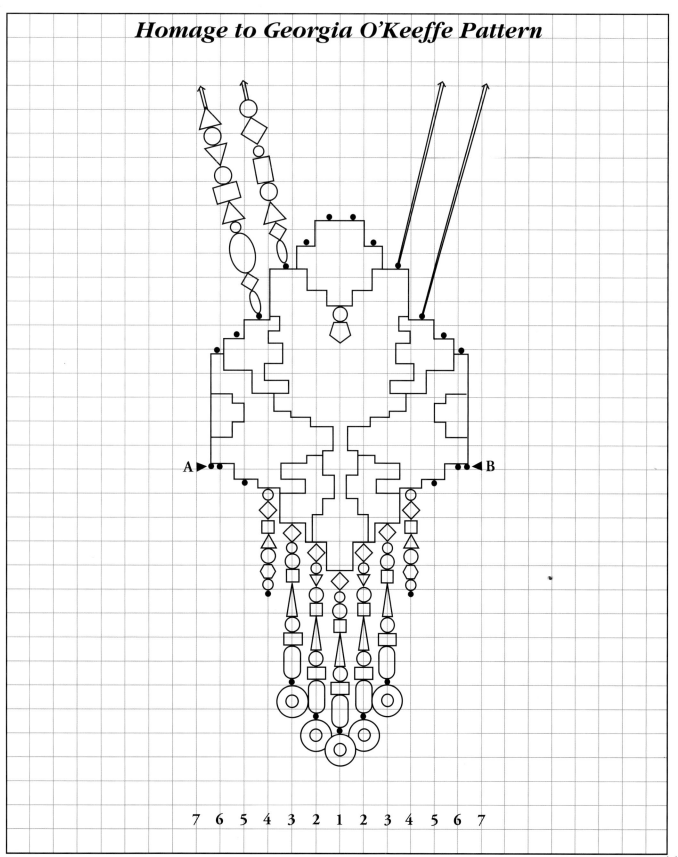

A◄ ►B

7 6 5 4 3 2 1 2 3 4 5 6 7

Color

There are many theories of color and numerous books are available that teach how to apply these theories to creating a successful necklace design. Since the necklace is a miniature work of art, color theories for works of art are applicable here. In a necklace, each shape should be clearly defined by a contrasting color, or the total effect will be a blur.

In order to simplify the terminology, I will use the basic terms: hue (the name of the color) and value (the lightness or darkness of the hue).

When I teach workshops for beginners, some students announce that they frequently wear black clothing and that therefore they will select black beads for their necklaces. I always have to explain that the dark areas of color and beads would be lost against a black background.

Since these necklaces can be worn on a variety of background colors, it is preferable to include light, medium, and dark values in a single piece to provide contrast against a range of clothing. The most effective contrast is created by placing the darkest value next to the lightest value.

Blue and White African Glass Beads: *This necklace combines dark, medium, and light values in a single piece. The darkest value is the denim blue-hued threads and glass beads; the medium value is the rust-hued threads; and the lightest value is the white-hued threads and glass beads. See Blue and White African Glass Beads Pattern on page 119.*

Blue and White African Glass Beads Pattern

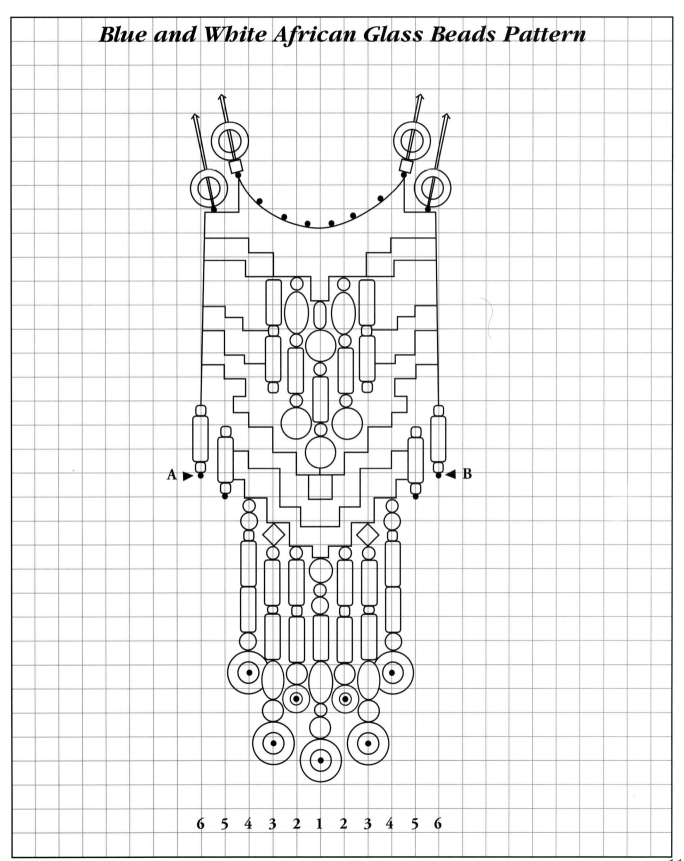

6 5 4 3 2 1 2 3 4 5 6

All That Glitters: *The brilliant variegated colors in each single bead made by René Roberts—ranging from blue to green to yellow to orange to red—demanded shining metallic threads combined with rayon to reflect the beads' luminescence.*

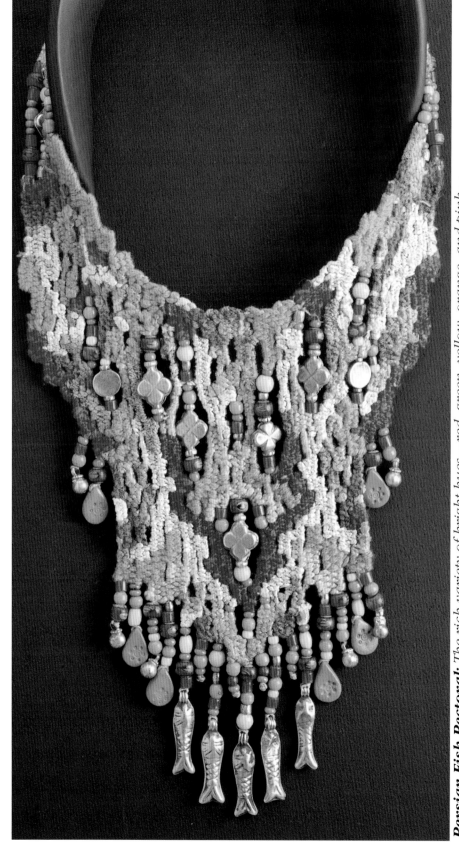

Persian Fish Pectoral: *The rich variety of bright hues—red, green, yellow, orange, and pink—provides a varied background for the soft silver dangles in the shape of fishes, from Iran.*

Texture

Texture provides tactile contrast between the soft flexible threads, the reflective glass beads, and the hard shine of the metal elements. You can enhance the jewel-like quality of the necklace by using metallic threads. When weaving with metallic threads*, I recommend #16 medium braid, which is available in many colors.

A shimmering effect can be created by weaving with two threads in the needle, combining a cotton or synthetic thread with a #8 fine metallic braid.

Texture can be achieved on the surfaces of gold pieces and polymer clay elements and can be emphasized with varying thicknesses of yarn. Variety may also be explored by using rayon, silk, mixtures of synthetic fibers, or any fiber that can be threaded through the eye of the needle.

Green Goddess:

The shimmering glass beads seemed to call out for luminous metallic and silk threads to surround them and gold and glass beads to accompany them. Dichroic glass beads made by René Roberts. See Green Goddess Pattern on page 123.

*Kreinik metallic thread is recommended and was used in these projects.

Green Goddess Pattern

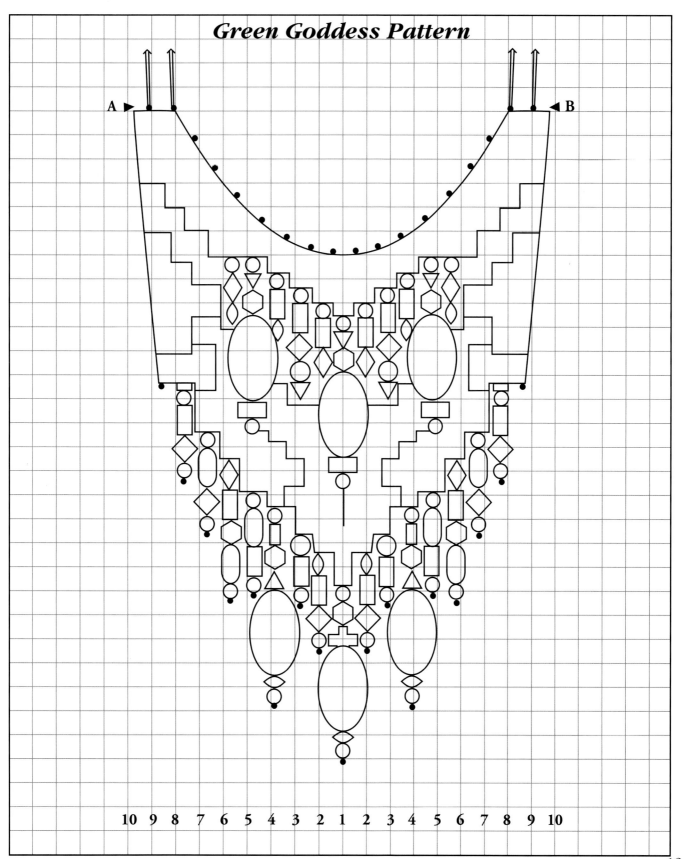

A ▶   ◀ B

10 9 8 7 6 5 4 3 2 1 2 3 4 5 6 7 8 9 10

Frivolous Fishes: *The textural effect of the long, loose strands of tubular threads flowing throughout the necklace add dimension and movement to the weaving. The carvings on the polymer clay fishes, made by Lee Meyers (sister of Helen Banes), add even more texture.*

Autumn Mood: *Symmetrical necklace with threads that provide a textural effect, combined with a variety of metal beads with reflecting surfaces.*

Bibliography

TECHNIQUES AND TEXTILES

Clark, Jill Nordfors. *Needle Lace: Techniques and Inspiration.* Madison, WI: Hand Books Press, 1999.

Dickens, Susan. *The Art of Tassel Making.* St. Leonards, NSW, Australia: Allen & Unwin, 1994.

Fisher, Nora, ed. *Mud, Mirror, and Thread: Folk Traditions of Rural India.* Ahmedabad: Mapin; Middletown, NJ: Grantha; Santa Fe, NM: Museum of New Mexico Press, 1993.

Fitzgerald, Diane, and Banes, Helen. *Beads and Threads: A New Technique for Fiber Jewelry.* Rockville, MD: Flower Valley Press, 1993.

Larson, Jack Lenor. *Interlacing: The Elemental Fabric.* Tokyo and New York: Kodansha, 1986.

Roche, Nan. *The New Clay.* Rockville, MD: Flower Valley Press, 1991.

BEADS

Benson, Ann. *Beadweaving: New Needle Techniques and Original Designs.* New York: Sterling, 1993.

Borel, France. *The Splendor of Ethnic Jewelry: From the Colette and Jean-Pierre Ghysels Collection.* New York: Harry N. Abrams, 1994.

Dubin, Lois Scherr. *The History of Beads: From 30,000 B.C. to the Present.* New York: Harry N. Abrams, 1987.

Liu, Robert K. *Collectible Beads: A Universal Aesthetic.* Vista, CA: Ornament, 1995.

Untracht, Oppi. *Traditional Jewelry of India.* New York: Harry N. Abrams, 1997.

AFRICAN INSPIRATIONS

Eyo, Ekpo, and Willett, Frank. *Treasures of Ancient Nigeria.* New York: Alfred A. Knopf, 1980.

Fagg, William. *Yoruba Beadwork: Art of Nigeria.* New York: Rizzoli, 1980.

Fisher, Angela. *Africa Adorned.* New York: Harry N. Abrams, 1984.

Hahner-Herzog, Iris, Kecskési, Maria, and Vajda, László. *African Masks: From the Barbier-Mueller Collection, Geneva.* Munich and New York: Prestel, 1998.

Meurant, Georges. *Shoowa Design: African Textiles from the Kingdom of Kuba.* New York: Thames and Hudson, 1986.

EGYPTIAN VISIONS

Aldred, Cyril. *Jewels of the Pharaohs: Egyptian Jewelry of the Dynastic Period.* New York: Praeger, 1971.

Andrews, Carol, *Ancient Egyptian Jewelry.* New York: Harry N. Abrams, 1991.

Edwards, I.E.S. *The Treasures of Tutankhamun.* New York: Metropolitan Museum of Art, 1976.

Wilson, Eva. *Ancient Egyptian Designs for Artists and Craftspeople.* London: British Museum, 1986.

CHINESE AND NEPALESE INFLUENCES

Fairservis, Walter A., Jr. *Costumes of the East.* Riverside, CT: Chatham Press, 1971.

Gabriel, Hannelore. *The Jewelry of Nepal.* New York: Weatherhill, 1999.

Garrett, Valery M. *Mandarin Squares: Mandarins and Their Insignia.* Hong Kong and New York: Oxford University Press, 1990.

Hansen, Henny Harold. *Mongol Costumes.* London and New York: Thames and Hudson, 1994.

Williams, C.A.S. *Outlines of Chinese Symbolism and Art Motives.* New York: Dover, 1976.

PRE-COLOMBIAN AND LATIN AMERICAN INFLUENCES

Davis, Mary L., and Pack, Greta. *Mexican Jewelry.* Austin, TX: University of Texas Press, 1963.

Lechuga, Ruth D., and Sayer, Chloë. *Mask Arts of Mexico.* San Francisco: Chronicle Books, 1995.

Reid, James W. *Textile Masterpieces of Ancient Peru.* New York: Dover, 1986.

Schele, Linda, and Miller, Mary Ellen. *The Blood of Kings: Dynasty and Ritual of Maya Art*. New York: George Braziller; Fort Worth, TX: Kimbell Art Museum, 1986.

Tushingham, A.D. *Gold for the Gods: A Catalogue of an Exhibition of Pre-Inca and Inca Gold and Artifacts from Peru*. Toronto: Royal Ontario Museum, 1976.

NATIVE AMERICAN INFLUENCES

Dockstader, Frederick J. *Weaving Arts of the North American Indians*. Rev. ed. New York: IconEditions, 1993.

Dubin, Lois Scherr. *North American Indian Jewelry and Adornment: From Pre-History to the Present*. New York: Harry N. Abrams, 1999.

Fienup-Riordan, Ann. *The Living Tradition of Yup'ik Masks: Agayuliyararput—Our Way of Making Prayer*. Seattle: University of Washington Press, 1996.

Furst, Peter, and Furst, Jill. *North American Indian Art*. New York: Rizzoli, 1982.

Mather, Christine. *Native America: Arts, Traditions, and Celebrations*. New York: Clarkson Potter, 1990.

ART NOUVEAU AND ART DECO STYLE

Gillon, Edmund V. *Art Nouveau: An Anthology of Art and Design from the Studio*. New York: Dover, 1969.

Hull, John. *Art Deco*. San Francisco: Troubador Press, 1975.

René Lalique. *The Jewels of Lalique*. Ed. Yvonne Brunhammer. Paris and New York: Flammarion, 1998.

Lesieutre, Alain. *The Spirit and Splendour of Art Deco*. New York: Paddington Press, 1974.

PERIODICALS

Bead and Button

Fiber Arts

Lapidary Journal

Ornament

Threads

Metric Conversions

INCHES TO MILLIMETRES AND CENTIMETRES

INCHES	MM	CM	INCHES	CM	INCHES	CM
1/8	3	0.9	9	22.9	30	76.2
1/4	6	0.6	10	25.4	31	78.7
3/8	10	1.0	11	27.9	32	81.3
1/2	13	1.3	12	30.5	33	83.8
5/8	16	1.6	13	33.0	34	86.4
3/4	19	1.9	14	35.6	35	88.9
7/8	22	2.2	15	38.1	36	91.4
1	25	2.5	16	40.6	37	94.0
1 1/4	32	3.2	17	43.2	38	96.5
1 1/2	38	3.8	18	45.7	39	99.1
1 3/4	44	4.4	19	48.3	40	101.6
2	51	5.1	20	50.8	41	104.1
2 1/2	64	6.4	21	53.3	42	106.7
3	76	7.6	22	55.9	43	109.2
3 1/2	89	8.9	23	58.4	44	111.8
4	102	10.2	24	61.0	45	114.3
4 1/2	114	11.4	25	63.5	46	116.8
5	127	12.7	26	66.0	47	119.4
6	152	15.2	27	68.6	48	121.9
7	178	17.8	28	71.1	49	124.5
8	203	20.3	29	73.7	50	127.0

Index